Haddon Hall

Geo. Cross, Photo] HADDON HALL FROM THE MEADOWS.

Haddon Hall

An Illustrated Account of the Fabric and its History

BY

F. H. CHEETHAM,

Author of

"Architectural and Historical Notes on Haddon Hall."

"Whoso is hungry and list well eate
Let him come to Haddon to his meate,
And for a night and for a daye
His horse shall have both corne and haye,
And no man shall ask hym when he goeth away."

Old Ballad

SHERRATT AND HUGHES

LONDON: 35 LONG ACRE W.

MANCHESTER: 27 ST. ANN STREET

1904

ISBN 1 873775 008

Reprinted in 1991 for

Ashbourne Editions
Clifton, Ashbourne, Derbyshire

Printed in the UK by:
Antony Rowe Ltd, Chippenham

To

E. E.,

G. R. E.,

&

E. W.,

"Compagnons de voyage."

PREFACE.

THIS book does not in any way aim at presenting a detailed archæological description of Haddon Hall. It is meant for a class of reader for whom a technical and exhaustive monograph, such as I hope will some day be written on Haddon Hall, could scarcely appeal. It merely seeks to do in some measure for Haddon what has been done so well for our Cathedral Churches by Messrs. Bell in their "Cathedral Series." That is to say an attempt has been made "to supply visitors with an accurate and well-illustrated guide book compiled with sufficient knowledge and scholarship to be of value to the student of archæology and history, and yet not too technical in language for the use of an ordinary visitor or tourist."

Haddon Hall is one of the best known of the old baronial houses of England. This, no doubt, is owing largely to its being situated in the centre of a district much frequented by tourists on account of its natural beauty, but much is also owing to the public spirit of successive Dukes of Rutland who have at all times generously thrown open the house for inspection to visitors.

There are naturally many guide books dealing at greater or less length with Haddon Hall, but as far as I am aware there is no single book that gives a really complete and fully-illustrated account of the building. There is little that is new in the following pages, but the information here presented to the reader has been brought together from sources that are scattered, and not easily accessible to those for whom the book is primarily intended. The principal of these sources are indicated in the bibliography at the end of the volume.

The confusion existing in nearly all accounts of Haddon Hall in regard to the early history of its lords has been removed by the late Mr. W. A. Carrington, of Bakewell, whose paper on the Family Record of Haddon I have taken as the final word on this subject, and whose kindness in placing at my disposal much information which he alone possessed I wish here to put on record. Mr. Carrington's death, in February of the present year, was a great blow to all who love Haddon, and his loss will be greatly felt throughout Derbyshire.

The plans in this book are based on those in Lysons' "Magna Britannia," which were prepared by the surveyor of the fifth Duke of Rutland to illustrate a privately printed account of the building written by the Duke, and show two floors of the house. These comprise practically all the rooms on the south, west, and east sides of the building, but on the north side (towards Bakewell) there is a basement and a second floor which are not shown on these plans, and the upper rooms in the towers are, of course, not indicated.

Haddon Hall has been the subject of much attention at the hands of writers of fiction. This is, of course, largely owing to the story of Dorothy Vernon which is the one piece of romance connected with the building. But apart from this Haddon has certain literary claims to attention. Rhodes, in his "Peak Scenery," tells us that "Mrs. Ann Radcliffe, who was a native of Derbyshire, often visited Haddon Hall, for the purpose of storing her imagination with those romantic ideas, and impressing upon it those sublime and awful pictures which she so much delighted to portray: some of the most gloomy scenery of her 'Mysteries of Udolpho' was studied within the walls of this ancient structure."

In "Peveril of the Peak" there is a note relating to the arrangements of the apartments in Martindale Castle which has been the excuse for inserting in some of the illustrated editions of the Waverley Novels a picture of Haddon Hall as representing Martindale Castle. The note, which, as Mr. Cokayne pointed out long ago, is sheer nonsense, reads as follows: "This peculiar collocation of apartments may be seen at Haddon Hall, Derbyshire, once a seat of the Vernons, where, in the lady's pew in the chapel, there is a sort of scuttle, which opens into the kitchen, so that the good lady could ever and anon, without much interruption of her religious duties, give an eye that the roast meat was not permitted to burn, and that the turnbroche did his duty." Such an experience at

Haddon Hall is simply impossible, for the chapel is in the south-west corner and the kitchen far away on the north side. It is high time this note in "Peveril of the Peak" was withdrawn.

The Baroness de Calabrella's "Evenings at Haddon Hall" (1846) has little to do with the building except as regards the title. It is a collection of tales supposed to have been told there, written round a number of steel engravings—not of Haddon—after drawings by George Cattermole. The story of Dorothy Vernon has been made the subject of several novels and tales, amongst which may be mentioned: "The King of the Peak," by William Bennett (1823, re-issued 1883); "Dorothy Vernon of Haddon Hall," by Charles Major (1902); "Sweet 'Doll' of Haddon Hall," by J. E. Muddock (1903); "Doll, a dream of Haddon Hall," by J. E. Muddock; and "The Heiress of Haddon," by W. E. Doubleday. "Haddon Hall," an opera by Sydney Grundy and Arthur Sullivan was produced in 1892, and is founded on the love story of Dorothy Vernon.

I have to acknowledge with sincere thanks my indebtedness to Mr. Henry A. Rye, architect, of Bakewell, who has given me much valuable information concerning the fabric under his charge, and who has been good enough to read through the proof-sheets and make various suggestions and additions. To Mr. Eades, the custodian of Haddon, I desire to express my thanks for the courtesy I have always received at his hands. My thanks are also due to Messrs. E. Earnshaw and H. Langman for help in preparing the plans, and to Mr. J. R. Wigfull for the use of those of the photographs which bear his name.

F. H. CHEETHAM.

SOUTHPORT,
June, 1904.

CONTENTS.

LIST OF ILLUSTRATIONS.

List of Illustrations

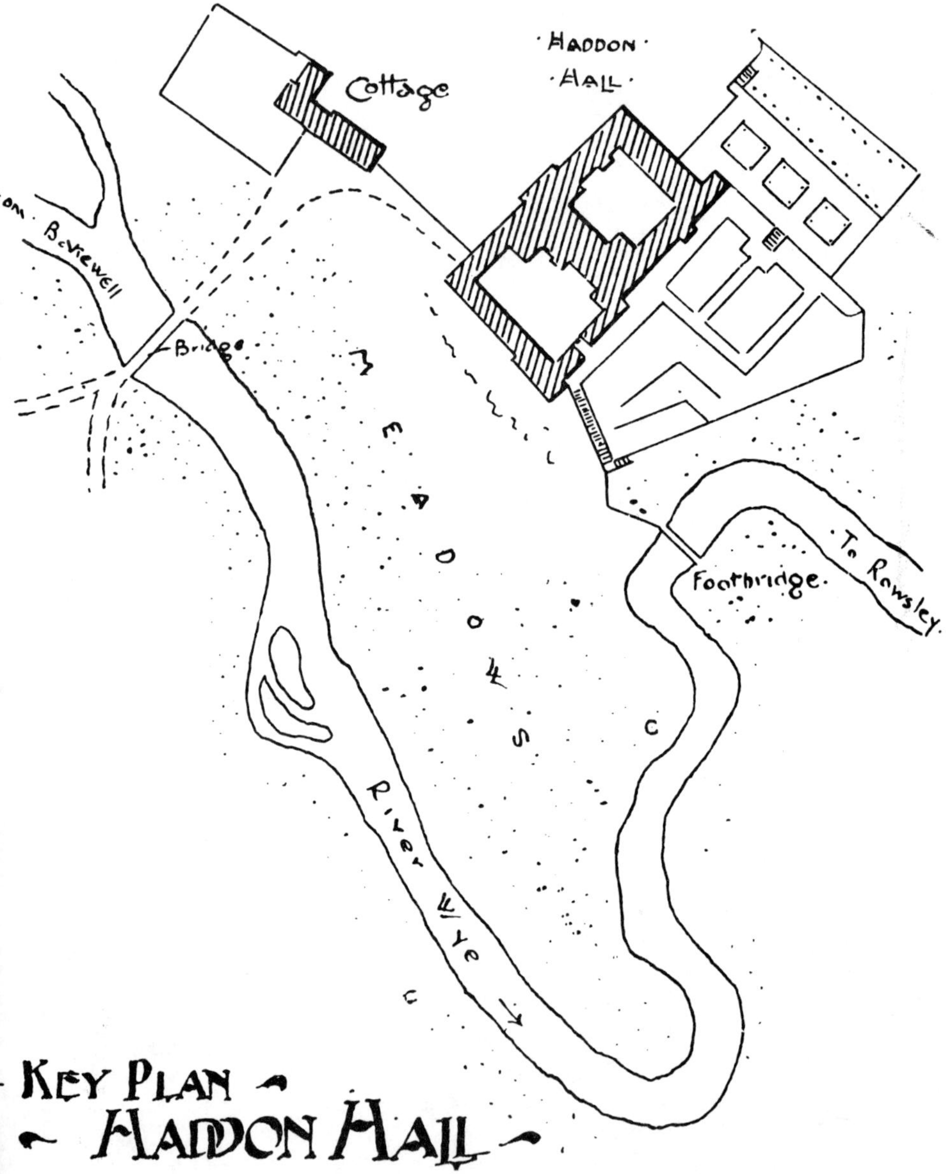

KEY PLAN HADDON HALL

HADDON HALL

CHAPTER I.—HISTORY OF THE BUILDING.

Where harmony results
From disunited parts; and shapes minute,
At once distinct and blended, boldly form
One vast majestic whole.
WILLIAM MASON.

HADDON[1] HALL is situated about two miles south-east of the town of Bakewell, in the county of Derby.

There is much difficulty in writing a history of the building, as the records of the early owners of Haddon are scanty, and give little information concerning the erection of the house, or any part of it. The dates assigned to the various portions of the structure cannot be stated with any degree of certainty, and, until we reach the sixteenth century, must be to a large extent a subject for speculation and theory.

It seems to have been too often assumed that

1 HADDON (Hadun, Haduna).—"The prefix is probably from the personal name Hadda, from A.S. aettox, aetter, naeddre—an adder, a snake, serpent, viper; or perhaps from A.S. haerh—heath or heather; the final syllable is A.S. dun—a mountain, hill, downs; Hadda's or the heather hill or downs. Dun is a word adopted by the Saxons from the Celts, and originally signified a hill-fortres, or stronghold."—*Etymology of some Derbyshire Place-names*, by Frederick Davis.

Haddon Hall was built on some pre-arranged plan round two courtyards, but in reality there is nothing to show that those who built the older portions of the mansion conceived of its final completion as we see it to-day. Rather is there evidence to make us believe that the ideas of one set of builders were rejected and put aside by those of a succeeding generation. The uniformity of appearance in the different parts of Haddon Hall must be ascribed to accident and local causes rather than to any premeditated scheme on the part of the first builders.

The house now stands alone and silent, an isolated building. But it grew to its present shape in the centre of what we may suppose to have been an active community, the vill of Nether Haddon. There are still a few cottages in its immediate vicinity, but most of them have disappeared. We have, then, the question to face as to whether in its early days the area occupied by the present building was occupied by one great dwelling only or by more than one.

The first mention of Haddon is in Domesday Book, where there is the following reference to Bakewell:—

"In Badequella (Bakewell) with eight berewicks, King Edward had eighteen carucates of land to be taxed. Land to eighteen ploughs. The King has now there in the demesne seven ploughs, and thirty-three villeins and nine bordars. There are two priests and a church, and under them two villeins and five bordars, all these having eleven ploughs. There is one knight having sixteen acres of land and two bordars. There is one mill of ten shillings and eightpence, and one lead mine, and eighty acres of meadow. Coppice wood one mile long and one broad. Three carucates of that land belong to the church. Henry de Ferrieres claims one carucate in Hadune. The berewicks of this manor are: Hadun, Holun, Reuslege, Burtune, Cranchesberie, Aneise, Maneis, Haduna."

The modern names of these berewicks have been assigned as Haddon, Holme, Rowsley, Burton, Conkesbury, One Ash, Monyash, and Haddon. The recurrence of the name Haddon is accounted for by there being two places of that name, Over Haddon and Nether Haddon. It is in the latter of these that Haddon Hall is situated.

From the Domesday survey, therefore, we see that Haddon was at that time a berewick[1] in the Royal Manor of Bakewell, and further that Henry

1 BEREWICK.—" Its name seems to signify primarily a wick, or village, in which barley is grown; but like the barton (bertona) and the grange (grangia) of later days, it seems often to be a detached portion of a manor which is in part dependent on, and yet in part independent of, the main body. Probably at the berewick the lord has some demesne land and some farm buildings, a barn or the like, and the villeins of the berewick are but seldom called upon to leave its limits; but the lord has no hall there, he does not consume its produce upon the spot, and yet for some important purposes the berewick is a part of the manor. The berewick might well be some way from the hall; a manor in Hampshire had three berewicks on the mainland and two in the Isle of Wight."—*Domesday Book and Beyond*, by F. W. Maitland.

de Ferrieres claimed one carucate[1] there. The Manor[2] of Bakewell was parcel of the ancient demesnes of the Crown, and was bestowed by William the Conqueror, along with other extensive estates, on his natural son William Peverel, known subsequently as Peverel of the Peak. Peverel is, therefore, the first "lord of Haddon" of whom there is any authentic record. Whether or not any building stood on the site of Haddon Hall prior to the time of the Conquest cannot now be determined. Bakewell was undoubtedly known to the Romans, who worked the lead mines there and in the neighbourhood, and there can be little doubt that the mineral waters from which Bakewell takes its name[3] were known to them. A Roman altar has

1 CARUCATE.—"In the financial system the carucate plays in the counties of Derby, Nottingham, and Leicester, the part that is played for others by the hide. The carucate has for its eighth part the bovate. These terms seem to be French: that is to say, they apparently formed no part of the official Latin that had been current in England. We do not know what the English jurors said when the Norman clerks wrote carucate and bovate; perhaps plough-gate, and ox-gate, or plough-gang and ox-gang; or, again, a plough of land, for these were the vernacular words of a later age. The hide and carucate seem to have been fiscally equivalent, and to have consisted of 120 acres."—*Domesday Book and Beyond*, by F. W. Maitland.

2 "A manor is a house against which geld (a land-tax of so much per hide or carucate) is charged. The hall is the place where geld is demanded and paid. A manor without a hall is a thing to be carefully noted otherwise some geld may be lost."—*Ibid.*

3 'Bake' a contraction of the Anglo-Saxon word *bedican*, protected with a dike. Bedican-well, the bediked well, there being a mineral spring at that place.—*Traces of History in the Names of Places*, by Flavell Edmunds, p. 170.

been found between Haddon and Bakewell, though there is no trace of Haddon's ever having been a Roman station. "The first mention we find of this town (Bakewell)," says Lysons, "is in the reign of Edward the Elder, who, as we are told in the Saxon Chronicle, marched with his army in the year 924 from Nottingham to Badecanwillan, and there commanded a castle to be built in its neighbourhood and garrisoned." This castle stood on the summit of what is now called Castle Hill, where the remains of ancient earthworks may yet be traced. The fact of Bakewell being at so early a date a place of importance lends probability to the belief expressed by Duesbury that the oldest portions of the present building at Haddon had an antecedent, as the site would naturally commend itself.

The Domesday survey was commenced in 1081, and the Conqueror died in 1087. The grant of the manor of Bakewell to William Peverel must have taken place, therefore, sometime between these two dates, it being necessarily subsequent to the year in which the survey of Derbyshire took place. Peverel at that time had large possessions in the county, but they did not include Bakewell. Henry de Ferrieres, or Ferrers, was also largely possessed of lands in Derbyshire, and at a later date the families of Peverel and Ferrieres intermarried.

William Peverel is said to have been the son of the Conqueror by the daughter of Ingelric, founder of the Collegiate Church of St. Martin's-le-Grand, London, but the only authority for this statement seems to be Richard Glover, Somerset Herald, quoted by Sir William Dugdale. The lady's name is doubtful, but was probably Maud, and all that is known either of her or her father is vague and contradictory.[1] The connexion of William of Normandy with the daughter of Ingelric probably took place when the former made a visit to King Edward the Confessor in 1048,[2] but whether the lady was then married or whether she married subsequently cannot be determined. Her husband was one Ranulf Peverel, and it has been stated, but without sufficient authority, that she obtained the consent of her husband that this son, whom she had previously presented to the King, should bear the name of Peverel also. What is certain is that the issue of Maud by the Conqueror took the name of her husband.

William Peverel, the son of the Conqueror, possessed sixteen manors in Derbyshire, the castle of Nottingham, and Peak Castle, at Castleton. He founded the priory of Lenton, near Nottingham, and died in 1113. His son, also named William Peverel, is said to have predeceased him, but all these records of the Peverels are so contradictory and confusing as to leave very little that can be accepted positively.

[1] Planché. [2] Rayner.

The Peverels held the manor of Haddon along with that of Bakewell for about seventy years. In 1154 or 1155 a William Peverel was deprived of his possessions by Henry II. on that monarch's ascending the throne. Dugdale calls this William the son of the first, but it is possible that he was the grandson of the Conqueror's son. Camden says: "William Peverel, lord of Nottingham, had a son of the same name, who died during his father's lifetime, and he had likewise a son William deprived of his estates by Henry II. for combining with the wife of Ranulf, Earl of Chester . . . to poison the said earl her husband."

However this may be, that Peverel was disinherited for poisoning the Earl of Chester is stated distinctly by such authorities as Matthew Paris, Matthew of Westminster, Gervase of Dover, the register of Dunstable, and the Chronican Roffense.[1] The story goes that fearing the rigour of the king he betook himself to the monastery at Lenton, of which he was patron, where he assumed the monastic habit, but on Henry's journey north to York, not feeling himself safe there he again fled, and is not afterwards heard of. His lands were then confiscated.

But Mr. Planché has pointed out that before Henry ascended the throne, probably in 1152, certainly not later than 1153, he gave to Ranulf, Earl of Chester, the castle and town of Nottingham

1 Planché.

and the whole fee of William Peverel, unless he, Peverel, could acquit and clear himself of his "wickedness and treason" (scelere et proditione). Peverel had been a strong partizan of King Stephen during that Monarch's wars with Henry and his mother, the Empress Maud, and at one time Maud had taken and held his castle at Nottingham. We might be justified, then, in believing that Peverel lost his estates not for assisting to poison the Earl of Chester, but for "wickedness and treason" generally, in plain words, for supporting Stephen manfully and faithfully against Henry and his mother.[1]

Most of the lands and honours of Peverel, including the manor and church of Bakewell reverted to the Crown, and were given by Henry to his son John, Earl of Mortaign, afterwards King John. In the first year of his reign John granted the manor or fee of Bakewell to Ralph Gernon, whose descendants remained lords of Bakewell till the beginning of the sixteenth century.

Haddon, or Nether Haddon, which at the time of the Domesday survey was a berewick, appertaining to the lordship of Bakewell, had been granted by Peverel to one of his retainers named Avenel, on tenure of knight's service. The Avenels were a Norman family, hereditary seneschals of the Counts of Mortaine. William the Seneschal

1 *Journal of the British Archæological Association*, vol. viii.

Geo. Cross, Photo]　HADDON HALL FROM THE NORTH-WEST.

came over with the Conqueror and fought at Hastings, but he does not appear to have been as richly rewarded for his services as some other of the Conqueror's companions.

The flight and outlawry of Peverel, while causing the forfeiture to the Crown of all such estates as were in his uncontrolled possession, had not that effect on those of his lands or manors which had been bestowed on his dependents. And so while the manor of Bakewell passes to the Crown, Haddon continues in the possession of Peverel's under-tenants, the Avenels. The granting of lands to military retainers, to be held by knights' service, was a general practice among the great barons in the reigns of the Norman Kings, and it seems that when the original grantors forfeited their own estates by reason of treason or felony, their military tenants, if they had not been implicated in their crimes, did not share in the punishment. They were only affected in so far as they had to transfer their homage from the baron to the sovereign.

The manor of Haddon, therefore, separate from that of Bakewell, passed to the Avenels as under-tenants of the Crown at the beginning of the reign of Henry II. The records of the Avenels are scanty and unimportant, and very little is known of them except that they held Haddon for about forty years. The last of them, William Avenel, left two daughters, co-heiresses, Avice and Elizabeth, who married respectively Richard de Vernon and Simon Basset.

There is no record of any building at Haddon during these early years of the Peverels. There is no reason to suppose that the Peverels ever resided at Haddon, but it is not unreasonable to conjecture that they were the builders of the oldest portions of the existing structure. Mr. Duesbury writes:

"The first thing Peverel of the Peak would do would be to build himself a tower of strength, or castle, if he did not find one already built, the keep of which was probably on the site of the present north-east tower, and I am inclined to think some portions of the old walls still remain. . . . The south side of the chapel is undoubtedly Norman, although it has been altered and modified; and I fancy I have discovered traces of early foundations along the north and west fronts, but the nature of the construction makes it impossible to decide. Our only certainty is the chapel; and supposing it to have been originally built as a chapel, we may fairly conjecture the place was of some importance to justify such an appendage; but if it were a place of importance it is remarkable that further traces of it do not remain, especially as it never appears to have been attacked or destroyed in warfare. It was the residence of families of high standing for 120 or 130 years, and although the Peverels held Nottingham Castle, a magnificent place then newly built, and chiefly resided there, still the Avenels were a great family and would require a suitable abode; but what it was there is nothing left to tell. Upon the whole, I am inclined to think that a space equal to the present area covered by the building was walled in, to which tenants and retainers could retire for protection with their families and cattle in case of attack, the house, or hall and offices, being within the walls."

The fact that so few traces of this early building remain is not perhaps so remarkable as at first sight it may appear when it is considered that the site on which Haddon Hall stands is a very confined one. It is only natural that the older building should have disappeared in order to give place to later work as the life and requirements of the times altered.

If the original house stood on the site of the north-east tower it seems strange that the chapel should be situated so far away. It must be remembered, however, that this chapel served as the parish church of the vill[1] of Nether Haddon, and there is indeed nothing positively to prove that in the first instance, at the time when the Norman work was erected, the chapel was specially an appendage to the castle, or house, of the lords of Haddon.

1 "The 'vill.' or 'town' of the later middle ages was, like the civil parish of our day, a tract of land with some houses on it, and this tract was a unit in the national system of police and finance."—*Domesday Book and Beyond*, by F. W. Maitland.

The difficulty of forming an opinion as to the extent and character of the first building is increased by reason of our ignorance as to the size, importance, and extent of the village of Nether Haddon. Did it lie altogether outside of the limestone platform which the present mansion wholly occupies, or did part of it stand on that platform, disappearing eventually in the extension of the great house? It seems reasonable to suppose that in early days the dwelling of the lords of Haddon would occupy only a small portion of the present area of Haddon Hall, but what the precise disposition of the buildings on this area then was we shall probably never determine.

The earliest record at present known concerning Haddon is a charter in the possession of the Duke of Rutland setting forth an agreement between William Avenel of Haddon and his two sons-in-law, Richard de Vernon and Simon Basset. A translation of a portion of this deed reads as follows:

"Be it known to all, as well present as to come, that I, William Avenel, have entered into an agreement with Richard de Vernon and Simon Basset, who have my two daughters and heirs, of all my land and inheritance, and to them as my heirs, I have granted and enfeoffed all my land and inheritance after my decease, which they shall divide, sharing equally everywhere. . . Moreover, in my manor, namely, Haddon, I have granted to the aforesaid Richard my capital mansion, which is on the east, where my father, William Avenel dwelt, and where the chapel of S. Nicholas is founded, with the orchard on the same side, and to Simon Basset my other mansion, which is at the west, with the orchard on that west side."

This deed has been conjecturally dated about 1170. The family of Basset, says Mr. Carrington, continued to possess a moiety of Nether Haddon in the reign of Edward III., but in or before the reign of Henry VI. it became vested by purchase in the Vernons. These two mansions in Nether Haddon, it may be safely conjectured, were on the site of the present building, the orchards occupying what are now the two courtyards. The great hall may have been common to both, or a second hall may have existed. But before anything can be authoritatively decided as to the actual disposition of the buildings at the time of the death of William Avenel, further results of the archæological investigation of the building, now proceeding, must be awaited.

It has been suggested that the second, or western mansion, lay outside the line of the present building as the "capital mansion in the east" is designated as being "where the chapel of S. Nicholas is founded," and the east side of the actual site is that farthest away from the chapel, which occupies the south-west angle. But the expression "in the east, where the chapel of S. Nicholas is founded," in all probability refers to the site of both mansions in regard to their position in the manor of Nether Haddon. Haddon Hall lies near the eastern border of the manor, which stretches westward as far as the River Lathkill, and nowhere within the limits of the manor in this direction is there sign or indication of anything answering to the description of a mansion. Why the Bassets, if they occupied part of the building on the present site, have left no trace of their occupation behind it is difficult to say. They were probably a declining family, and may, indeed, have possessed the moiety of Haddon without occupying the house there. At any rate, the Vernons seem to have been looked upon as lords of Haddon from the time of the first Sir Richard, the husband of Avicia Avenel. The two houses seem to have been gradually merged into one, which was the Vernon's. But the whole of this early history is still very obscure.

Haddon Hall is essentially the Vernon's building. Apart from the south aisle of the chapel and some old walls perhaps incorporated in the north-east tower, no part of the present building can be assigned to a date earlier than that of the first Vernon, and it was Sir George, the last of the line, who practically completed the structure. All the subsequent work of the Manners in the seventeenth

Geo. Cross, Photo]

THE GARDEN FRONT.

century is more in the way of embellishing and furnishing than in actual building.

The Vernons were an ancient family from Normandy, who derived their name from the chatellanie of Vernon, now a town in the department of the Eure, between Rouen and Paris. The Vernon who came over with the Conqueror was rewarded with the manor of Shipbrook, in Cheshire, which became the principal seat of the family. By means of advantageous marriages, or Royal grants, different members of this family obtained establishments in some of the adjacent counties, especially in Derbyshire. The early history of the Vernons, both before and after their establishment as lords of Haddon, is involved and very difficult to unravel. The late Mr. W. A. Carrington, curator of the Duke of Rutland's manuscripts at Belvoir, himself a descendant of the Vernons, and probably the best authority on the genealogy of the family, admits that "although many attempts have been made from time to time to elucidate the family history, yet, with the result of these investigations, it will be found that still at the present no two authorities are agreed. One of the principal difficulties in regard to the Vernon genealogy arises from the prevalence of Richards, which renders it difficult to distinguish one from another, as seven Richards occur from the first, who married Avice Avenel, in the latter half of the twelfth century, until the year 1450. The marriages of these Richards have been a source of much perplexity, sometimes the father and son being assigned to the same wife."[1]

Sir Richard Vernon, the first lord of Haddon, was probably a great grandson of the first baron of Shipbrook. Most likely from the time that he obtained an estate at Haddon he and his descendants made it their family seat and chief residence.

The next definite record concerning Haddon is a licence or writ directed by John, Earl of Mortaign (afterwards King John) to his justices, sheriffs, bailiffs, ministers, and all his lieges, licensing Richard de Vernon to strengthen his house of Haddon with a wall to the height of twelve feet, without kernel (sine kernello), and forbidding him to be disturbed in so doing. It is attested at Clipston (a Royal Manor near to Market Harborough), but without a note of the time. John was then probably acting as regent in the absence of his brother King Richard in the Holy Land. The licence is endorsed "A writ patent of the earl John." It reads as follows:

"Johannis com. Moret. justic. vicecom. baillivis ministris et omnibus fidelibus suis salutem. Sciatis me concessisse et licenciam dedisse Ric. de Vern. firmande domum suum de Heddon muro exaltato xij pedibus sine kernello, et idem prohibeo

1 Derbyshire Archæological and Natural History Society's Journal. Vol. xxii., 1900.

nequis vestrum eum inde disturbet. Test. Rob. de Mara apud Clipeston.

Indorsed by a coeval hand. Breve patens com. Johannis."

The date of this writ is somewhere between the years 1190 and 1195, probably about 1193. The word "kernel," or "crenelle," sometimes signifies a battlement, but usually the embrasures of a battlement, or loopholes or other openings in the walls of a fortress, through which arrows and other missiles might be discharged against assailants. When a building was thus fortified it was said to be crenellated. It was necessary, however, to have a licence from the Crown to do this. But Haddon never had a licence to crenellate, and the fact that this wall had to be built "without kernel" shows that it was for protection only. A portion of this wall probably remains adjoining the east end of the chapel, the greater part of which is now under what is known as the Earl's Bedchamber and the adjoining apartments, and can only be seen from beneath (see p. 60). There are also remains of what is undoubtedly an ancient wall along the south and east fronts. The wall, however, immediately east of the chapel has corbels on both sides and was clearly isolated. If, then, this is really part of Sir Richard Vernon's wall, as seems most likely, it points to the probability that his house at Haddon occupied, at any rate on the south side, the whole of the space between the north east tower and the chapel.

Mr. Duesbury's surmise that in the time of the Avenels "a space equal to the present area covered by the building was walled in" did not therefore receive the emphatic confirmation that he claimed for it when the existence of this licence of the Earl of Mortaign was made known. The surrounding wall of which the deed gives record was built by Sir Richard Vernon, and there is nothing to suggest that it took the place of a formerly existing one.[1]

Sir Richard de Vernon was settled at Haddon in 1195. He was living in 1215, but was apparently dead before 1219. What he or his descendants did at Haddon for many years in the way of building there is no means of knowing. He was succeeded by his son William de Vernon.[2] The latter was living in 1237, and was probably identical with William de Vernon, chief justice of Chester in the reign of Henry III. He married Margaret, daughter of Sir Robert de Stokeport, Lord of Stockport, who brought to him the manor of Baslow and Bubnell. He probably married a second time, as a deed dated 1237 recites that "William de

1 Mr. Duesbury subsequently wrote: "I am inclined to think a wall existed originally, and that this grant referred more particularly to the raising of the wall." *Journal of the British Archæological Association.* Vol. vii.

2 See Carrington (Derbyshire Archæological and Natural History Society's Journal, Vol. xxii.), whose account of the Vernon genealogy is here followed.

Vernon, for the welfare of his soul, and the souls of his wife Alice and of all his ancestors and successors, had given all the land which he had in Stanton [near Haddon] to the prior and convent of Lenton, together with his body, there to be buried beside his father." William de Vernon died about 1242, and was succeeded by his son, Sir Richard de Vernon, Knt. He was alive in 1276, but dying without issue was succeeded by his brother Robert, who is supposed to have died shortly after.

The descent of Haddon and other possessions terminated in the male line of the Vernons with Robert de Vernon, who appears to have died without male issue, leaving an only daughter, Hawise, who married Gilbert le Franceys, who was afterwards knighted, but about whom little is known. He was dead in 1278. He left a son named Richard, born in 1261, who assumed his mother's name, and is thus known as Richard de Vernon. He married Isabel, daughter of Sir William Gernon, lord of Bakewell, by whom he had a son, likewise named Richard, who predeceased him in 1323. He was therefore succeeded by his grandson William de Vernon, born 1314, and he in his turn was succeeded by his son Sir Richard de Vernon.

This Sir Richard is the first of the early Vernons of Haddon of whom anything considerable is known, and the first who in any way helps us to determine the date of the erection of any of the buildings at Haddon Hall. In 1357 he assigns to his trustees "his manor of Haddon" prior to proceeding to the Holy Land, reserving to himself a right of re-entry if he returned to England. He evidently did return, as a later deed recites that "Sir Richard de Vernon is to go across the sea into Gascony in the service of our Lord the King [Edward III.]." He married Juliana, sister and heiress of Sir Fulk de Pembrugge, lord of Tong in Shropshire, by whom he acquired the manor of Tong.

Over the porch of the Great Hall are carved the arms of Vernon and Pembrugge, put there no doubt by this Sir Richard. This would fix the date of the porch somewhere between 1367, the approximate year of his marriage, and 1376, the year of his death. "The porch is, however, evidently an addition to the hall, which is of older date, assume that of Edward II., at which time also it is evident the chapel was restored, and the west window introduced. . . . Probably the works of the Great Hall were continuous, and comprised the Great Hall itself, the offices immediately adjoining the north end of it, the porch, and possibly the dining-room building. Most likely the parapets and battlements of the north-east tower were then restored." (Duesbury.)

The building of the Great Hall and offices may be assigned to the period between 1300 and 1380. The kitchen most likely stood where the present kitchen stands, but the whole northern range of

PORCH TO GREAT HALL.

buildings is of much later date, though it is very probable that the lower portion of the walls of the old kitchen was retained.

The next lord of Haddon is also named Richard de Vernon. He was the son of the last named, and was nine years of age at his father's death in 1376. He married Johanna, daughter of Rees ap Griffith, Knt., and died in 1400 at the age of thirty-two, leaving a son of the same name aged ten years.

This Richard de Vernon, born in 1390, became a man of some note. He probably served with Henry V. in France, and was knighted in 1418. He represented Derbyshire in the first Parliament of Henry VI., but in 1423 was in France. In 1425 he was High Sheriff of Derbyshire, and again represented the county in the Parliament which met at Leicester in 1426 (known as the Bats Parliament), where he was chosen Speaker of the House of Commons. He also held the offices of Captain of Rouen and Treasurer of Calais, which latter he resigned to his son shortly before his death in 1450. Sir Richard Vernon seems to have been a man of imperious disposition, for among a large number of manuscripts found at Belvoir Castle in 1885 by Mr. Maxwell-Lyte, was a long paper of complaints against him or his servants. He married Benedicta, daughter of Sir John Ludlow of Hodnet and Stokesay, Co. Salop, by whom he had a large family.

It was Sir Richard Vernon, the Speaker, who has left his name on the glass in the east window of the chapel, with the date 1427. The work at Haddon, which was probably finished before his death, consists of the eastern portion of the chapel, the rebuilding of the upper portion of the west end of the same, and the range of buildings on the east side of the upper court, between the north-east tower and the long gallery (Duesbury).

Sir Richard Vernon was succeeded at Haddon by his son, Sir William Vernon, born about 1420. He represented Derbyshire in three Parliaments, and had a grant of the office of Knight Constable of England for life. He married Margaret Pype, daughter and heiress of Sir Robert Pype and Spernore. The arms of Margaret Pype are introduced in the glass of the window in the south wall of the chapel. Sir William Vernon probably built the chapel turret. He died in 1467.

His second son, Sir Henry Vernon, who succeeded him, was twenty-six years of age at his father's death. He was a statesman and a man of letters, an astute man of great influence, courted in turn by Lancastrians and Yorkists. Among the papers found at Belvoir were several letters addressed to him in 1470 and 1471 by the Duke of Clarence and Edward IV. urging him to come to their assistance, and one dated March 25 [1471] from Richard, Earl of Warwick, the King Maker, heartily praying him to be with him at Coventry "with as many people defensibly arraied as ye can readily make," inasmuch as "yonder man Edward, the kinges oure soverain lord gret ennemy rebelle and traitour, is now late arrived in the north parties of this land and commyng fast on southward accompanyed with Flemynges, Esterlinges, and Danes." The letter bears the Earl's own signature and a remarkable postscript in his own hand: "Henry I pray you ffayle me not now as ever I may do ffor you." To quote from the late Duchess of Rutland's interesting account of these manuscripts: "We are not told what answer he returned to these letters, but he probably adopted the prudent course of staying quietly at home; for a few weeks later we again find several letters from the Duke of Clarence and Edward IV. addressed to him. On the 6th of May there is a letter from the Duke of Clarence giving an account of the battle of Tewkesbury, fought two days previously, and stating that 'Edward, late called Prince' was 'slain in plain battle,' which is the earliest extant authority upon the controverted question as to the manner in which the son of Henry VI. met his end."[1]

Sir Henry Vernon's attitude during the Wars of the Roses was one of non-interference. He seems to have enjoyed the confidence of both parties, but believed discretion to be the better part of valour. When Edward IV. was secure on the

[1] *Quarterly Review*, January, 1890.

throne we find Sir Henry Vernon as one of the squires of his body. He was a great favourite of Henry VII., and was appointed Governor and Treasurer to Prince Arthur, on whose creation as Prince of Wales in 1489 he was made a Knight of the Bath. According to tradition, Prince Arthur spent much of his time at Haddon with Sir Henry Vernon, and one of the apartments at the Hall, in the northern range of buildings, was known formerly as the "Prince's Chamber." Sir Henry witnessed the marriage contract between Prince Arthur and Katharine of Aragon. He represented Derbyshire in Parliament in 1478, and was High Sheriff of the county in 1504. He married Anne Talbot, daughter of the Earl of Shrewsbury, by whom he had a numerous family. His eldest son, John, died during his father's life-time, and is buried at Bakewell. His fourth son was the ancestor of the Lords Vernon of Sudbury. Sir Henry Vernon died in 1515, and was succeeded by his second son, Richard Vernon, who was "thirty years of age and upwards" at the death of his father. Richard married Margaret, daughter of Sir Robert Dimock, but was never knighted. He survived his father only a little over two years, dying in 1517.

Sir Henry Vernon probably continued the work of his predecessors at Haddon, and is credited with the erection of the western range of buildings, and to him is attributed the decoration of the ceiling in the Dining Room, which contains the Tudor arms and those of Talbot.

The western buildings were finished, however, by Sir George Vernon, the son of Richard, who came to the estates in 1517, when he was nine years old. Sir George Vernon was the last of the male Vernons who owned Haddon. He was twice married; first to Margaret, daughter of Sir Gilbert Talboys, by whom he had two daughters, Margaret and Dorothy, and second, to Maude, daughter of Sir Ralph Longford, by whom he had no issue. Camden says of him: "He was the last of this branch whose chief seat was at Haddon, by the river Wye, in Derbyshire, the seat for many years of the Vernons, who, as they were very ancient, so they were no less renowned in those parts, in so much as this Sir George Vernon, who lived in our times, for his magnificent port and hospitality, was called by the multitude *Petty King of the Peake*."

Sir George Vernon appears to have exercised great influence in the county, and his name occurs in 1565 amongst those "as are specially written unto the Lordes of the Counsell, to take care in the good assessing of the Subsidge." There are many stories extant of his hospitality, of his imperiousness, and of the power he held over the actions of those around him. One story, often told, may be repeated here. It is thus related by Mr. Jewitt:

"A pedlar who had been hawking his wares

in the neighbourhood was found murdered in a lonely spot. He had been seen the evening before to enter a cottage, and never afterwards seen alive. As soon as Sir George became aware of the fact of the crime having been committed, he had the body of the pedlar removed to Haddon, laid in the hall, and covered with a sheet. He then sent for the cottager to come immediately, and, on his arrival, at once questioned him as to where the pedlar was who was seen to enter his house the night before. The man denied having seen him or knowing anything about him, when Sir George uncovered the body before him, ordering that all persons present should touch the body in succession, at the same time declaring their innocence of the murder. The suspected man, when his turn came, declined to touch the body, and instantly rushed out of the hall, and made his way, 'as fast as his legs could carry him,' through Bakewell and towards Ashford. Sir George instantly ordered his men to mount and follow him, and to hang him wherever they caught him. The murderer was caught in a field opposite the toll-bar at Ashford, and at once hanged, and the field still bears the name of the 'Gallows Acre,' or 'Galley Acre.' Sir George is said to have been cited to London for this extraordinary piece of lynch law, and when he appeared in court he was summoned twice to surrender as 'the King of the Peak.' To these he made no reply, and the third time he was called on as Sir George Vernon, when he stepped forward and acknowledged himself: 'Here am I!' Having been summoned as the 'King of the Peak,' the indictment fell through, and Sir George was admonished and discharged."

Sir George Vernon died in 1567, and is buried at Bakewell. His vast possessions fell to his two daughters, both of whom were married in his lifetime, Margaret, the elder, to Sir Thomas Stanley, son of the third Earl of Derby, and Dorothy, the younger, to John Manners, second son of the Earl of Rutland. At the time of their father's death Margaret and Dorothy were aged twenty-six and twenty-one respectively. In the division of the property the Derbyshire estates, including Haddon Hall, fell to Dorothy, by whose marriage they passed into the hands of the Manners family.

Although some building was done at Haddon subsequent to the death of Sir George Vernon there can be little question but that the house had assumed very nearly its present form at that date. "Sir George not only finished the work of his predecessor," says Mr. Duesbury, "but his unbounded hospitality and mode of life prompted him to very materially add to them. It cannot now be ascertained whether any and what buildings occupied the site of the present range of offices in the north, or whether any important building occupied the site of the present long gallery, but there must have been some sort of kitchens and offices;

whatever they were, they do not appear to have been sufficient to enable Sir George to indulge in his princely hospitality, and to him I do not hesitate to ascribe the erection of the range of kitchens and offices which occupy nearly the whole of the north front; he also must have built the suite of rooms between the great hall and the chapel (although they are not entirely original, as traces of older works are remaining), and I have no doubt he altered the east range of buildings in the upper court, the bay-window of what is called the State Bed-chamber, being evidently an addition. . . . I am also inclined to believe that he built the walls of the long gallery as well as laid out the gardens."

Before referring to the work carried out at Haddon by John Manners, the husband of Dorothy Vernon, there is one point in the history of Haddon Hall during the Middle Ages, whilst it was the abode of the Vernons, which deserves notice. We have seen that the Vernons never had a licence to crenellate, and Haddon Hall was never, therefore, really a fortified dwelling. It has been said that its unfitness to be used for the purposes of war is the chief cause of its never being attacked. As it could not be used for purposes of aggression, it was never attacked, and throughout the whole course of its history there is no story of deeds of arms connected with it. Had there been so we might have had more light thrown on the history of the building, but what would have been gained in one direction would probably have been lost in another. Its immunity from the misfortunes of war has preserved it almost intact as a specimen of domestic architecture of the Middle Ages, unchanged except by the ravages of time and the alterations in the mode of life of its possessors. We have seen that in the troublous times of the Wars of the Roses Sir Henry Vernon stayed quietly at home, and the record of most of the lords of Haddon is that of duty done as members of Parliament, sheriffs of the county, governors of princes, and in like dignified employments.

The story, which is sometimes yet told, that the Sir Richard Vernon of Shakespeare's "King Henry IV." Part I., who was executed by order of the King after the battle of Shrewsbury in 1403, was one of the lords of Haddon, can be disproved by the fact that no owner of Haddon died in 1403. Moreover, as the late Duchess of Rutland has pointed out, the property of Haddon would have been confiscated had its owner been thus executed.

Everyone knows the romantic story of Dorothy Vernon's wooing and flight, but it cannot be passed over here. We have seen that Dorothy, the second daughter of Sir George Vernon, was married to John Manners before her father's death. The popular story runs that Dorothy had incurred the displeasure of her family by her attachment to John Manners, and that she was closely guarded in the house. Manners, however, being a very determined man and of a chivalrous disposition, disguised himself as a forester and lingered about the woods in the vicinity of Haddon, waiting till a favourable opportunity should occur to carry off the fair Dorothy. On the night of a grand feast and ball, given in honour of her sister's marriage to Sir Thomas Stanley, Dorothy is said to have quietly slipped out of the room where the revel was going on, made her way through an ante-room, and down the steps which now bear her name on to the terrace. From here she made her way through the gardens and down the long flight of steps by the chapel to the old footbridge across the river, where her lover was waiting for her with horses. They then galloped off through the night, and next day arrived at Aylestone, near Leicester, where they were married. Tradition adds that Sir George Vernon afterwards became quite reconciled to his daughter and son-in-law, so that all ended quite happily.

The details of this story, however, will not stand investigation. Although the long gallery, or ball-room, where the revel is supposed to have been held, was most likely finished in Sir George Vernon's days, there is no reason to believe that a door then existed where "Dorothy Vernon's Steps" are now situated. The terrace and gardens were not finished till many years after, by Dorothy's husband himself when he lived at Haddon, and the present

Geo. Cross, Photo]

"DOROTHY VERNON'S DOOR."

decoration of the long gallery, its panelling and ceiling, are also his work. Moreover, there is no reason to believe that John Manners was in any way an ineligible match for Dorothy Vernon. It is sometimes said that the stumbling-block was that the Vernons were Roman Catholics and the Manners Protestants. But apart from this there seems to be no reason why Sir George Vernon should have raised any objection. There is no evidence that he ever did so, and, according to the late Duchess of Rutland, "there is reason to believe that the King of the Peak was well satisfied with the alliance of the Vernons and the Manners."

Dorothy Vernon died in 1584, and is buried in Bakewell Church. Of her Mr. Jewitt writes: "It is said that she was one of the most beautiful of all beautiful women, and possessed of so sweet a temper that she was idolized by all who knew her. If it were so, however, the monument at Bakewell does not fairly represent her, for it exhibits her with an expression of countenance far from either amiable or attractive."

A good deal of light is thrown on the life at Haddon Hall during Sir George Vernon's day by the steward's accounts, which are still preserved, and from which a selection has been published by Mr. Carrington. These accounts extend, with some unfortunate blanks, from the year 1549 to past the middle of the seventeenth century. The entries during the times of Sir George Vernon confirm in every way the popular tradition as to the magnificent hospitality of the King of the Peak. There is not much, however, to help us regarding the erection of the building, though such items as the following give an indication of work in progress, and of repairs carried out. The date is 1549-50.

Itm payde the xxiiijth daye of Octobre unto Rycharde feylls of ouer haddon for iij dayes thatchynge of ye oxhowsse.	xij^{d}
It payde ye xvjth of november vnto Wyllm bowryngs wyffe for ye borde of henrye wagstafe Ryc. wyght Tomas noytte and Robarte handerton for iiij dayes workynge at Elkar for great Tymbre for ye howsse	ij^{s} viij^{d}
Ite payde vnto Rycharde wryght ye xijth of februarye for sawinge at haddon of bords for ye Carver & planks the qwantitye of thre Royds after fyeve shyllyngs ye Royde.	xv^{s}
Itm payde ye xxiijth of June vnto Robarte gladwhyne for Mendynge of ye glasse whyndowes in dyuers placs of ye howsse.	viij^{d}
It. payde ye xxvjth of June vnto to men for ye makynge & bornynge of ye lyme Kylne at haddon.	xij^{d}
It. payde ye xth of Julye vnto Tomas nycolsson for ye Makynge of a new fornys in ye brewhowsse at haddon.	x^{s}

John Manners, the husband of Dorothy Vernon, was the second son of the first Earl of Rutland. The family of Manners is said to have had its origin in Sir Robert Manners, Lord of the Manor of Ethall in Northumberland. In the days of Edward III. a Sir Robert Manners was governor of Norham Castle. In 1525 Henry VIII. bestowed upon Sir Thomas Manners the title of Earl of Rutland. The earl died in 1543, leaving five sons, the eldest of whom succeeded to the title, and the second was John Manners of Haddon. The earldom of Rutland did not come to the Haddon Manners till 1641, when, on the failure of the direct line, the title passed to the descendants of the second son of the first earl.

John Manners settled at Haddon on the death of his father-in-law in 1567. He was High Sheriff of Derbyshire in 1594, and appears to have been one of the gentlemen of landed property and influence who waited on King James to congratulate that monarch on his arrival from Scotland to ascend the throne of Great Britain. He had an interview with the new King at Worksop on April 20, 1603, when he was knighted. Three days afterwards his eldest son George was presented to King James at Belvoir and was likewise knighted. Sir John's wife, Dorothy, had been dead at this date nearly twenty years.

Sir John Manners died in 1611. The works in progress at Haddon at the time he succeeded to the estates were continued by him, and he probably lived to see the structure completed, for although some work about the house and grounds is later than his time it was more in the nature of repair and decoration than actual building. Mr. Duesbury states that "Sir John Manners finished the works in progress at the death of Sir George Vernon in 1567, that is, he decorated the long gallery with the very beautiful carved panelling and an ornamental ceiling, rich with coats of arms, amongst which those of Manners first appear. He finished the internal decorations of the state bedroom and of the rooms in the north-west or principal entrance tower."

How much of the later work at Haddon was done by Sir John Manners and how much by his two immediate successors is not certain. His son, Sir George Manners, died in 1623. The gardens, perhaps, had assumed something of their present aspect before this time. The terrace balustrade and steps are generally ascribed to Sir John Manners, but they may have been completed by his son. Sir George evidently re-roofed the chapel, and the pews and pulpit may have been put in by him, but this is rather doubtful (see p. 87). Sir George Manners is buried in Bakewell Church, where there is a fine monument to his memory. His son John Manners succeeded in 1641 to the earldom of Rutland on the death of his cousin, the seventh earl, who was childless. He united

J. R. Wigfull, Photo]

THE BRIDGE.

the two lines of the Manners family, and from this date Belvoir Castle, in Leicestershire, passes into the same ownership as Haddon Hall. The Earl of Rutland, however, lived mostly at Haddon, where he is said to have rivalled, if he did not surpass, the celebrated Sir George Vernon in his magnificent and lavish hospitality. He was one of the twenty-two peers who in January, 1642-3, declined to obey the King's summons to attend him at Oxford. The Manners family were on the side of the Parliament throughout the Civil War. Belvoir fell into the hands of the Royalists, but was recaptured in January, 1645-6, by the Parliamentary forces. The old castle was soon afterwards demolished. It is not surprising to find the Earl of Rutland living entirely at Haddon during the troublous times of the great rebellion. The even course of life at the Derbyshire house was apparently not much affected by the great struggle then going on. Just before the outbreak of hostilities, in June, 1642, a large number of muskets, carbines and other weapons was sent to Haddon from Belvoir, but the greater number appear to have been returned in the following October. Notwithstanding the part he had taken in the Civil War, the Earl of Rutland welcomed the restoration of Charles II., was favourably received by that monarch, and was made Lord Lieutenant of Derbyshire. He built the present bridge over the Wye at Haddon, and decorated the woodwork in some parts of the building. He died at Haddon in 1679, but is buried in Bottesford in Leicestershire.

John, ninth Earl and first Duke of Rutland, who succeeded his father in 1679, lived a good deal at Haddon, where much lavish hospitality was still maintained. He had been created a peer in his own right (Lord Manners of Haddon) shortly before his father's death, and in 1703 Queen Anne created him Marquis of Granby and Duke of Rutland. It was he who constructed the new bowling green on the hillside above Haddon. He died in 1711 at Belvoir.

Mr. Carrington says that the latest reference in the steward's accounts to the occupation of Haddon Hall by the family occurs in 1702, and that "it appears from the entries to have been a short visit." The late Duchess of Rutland states, however, that the third Duke, who succeeded to the title in 1721, and died in 1779, lived partly at Haddon. However that may be, it was certainly during his lifetime that the family finally quitted the Hall. The steward of the Rutland estates resided there for some years after 1702, and it may have been that the third Duke occasionally stayed there before the house was finally dismantled.

In the seventeenth century Haddon Hall was surrounded by a park of considerable extent, enclosed with wooden pales. In 1637 the park contained 597 bucks and does. Writing in 1782 Edward King says: "The great park that belonged to this house has been destroyed, and the land has been ploughed up, within these twelve years."

Fuller, in his account of Derbyshire, mentions "the fair pastures nigh Haddon . . . so incredibly battening (fattening) of cattle that one proffered to surround it with shillings to purchase it, which because to be set sideways, not edgeways, were refused."

The history of the building of Haddon Hall really comes to an end with the first quarter of the seventeenth century. The Manners have left their mark upon the house in the Renaissance spirit of the many details of their work. Most of the rain water pipes now existing were put up in their time, and they appear to have taken great care of the property. The only stable building remaining is that next to the custodian's cottage; others, near the same place, are said to have been pulled down about the end of the eighteenth century.

Before referring to the history of Haddon Hall in more recent days, it may be well to give here a resumé of the approximate dates of the different parts of the building. Mr. Duesbury divided the work at Haddon into five periods as follows:

First Period—about 1070 to (say) 1250.

The south aisle of the chapel. The walls, or some of them, of the north-east tower. Portions of walls in the south front. The wall under the Earl's apartments, east of the chapel.

Second Period—about 1300 to (say) 1380.

The great hall and offices. The hall porch. The lower west window of the chapel. Repairs to, and rebuilding of, portions of the north-east tower. Some work in the upper court under the long gallery.

Third Period—1380 to 1470.

The eastern portion of the chapel. Rebuilding of, and repairs to, the upper portion of the west end of the chapel. The buildings on the east side of the upper court.

Fourth Period—1470 to about 1550.

The fittings and finishing of the dining-room (the external works no doubt previously built). The western range of buildings. The western end of the north range (entrance tower, etc.).

Fifth Period—1550 to 1624 and onwards.

The northern range of buildings. The bay-window and other alterations to the eastern buildings in upper court. The staircase bay. The suite of rooms between the chapel and drawing-room known as the "Earl's apartments." The long gallery. The gardens and terrace. The pulpit, pews, and desk in the chapel. The stable and bowling green.

Since the beginning of the eighteenth century Haddon Hall has been uninhabited. When the dismantling process began such of the furniture as

Geo. Cross, Photo]

THE TERRACE STEPS.

was thought to be valuable was sent to Belvoir, but "that which was not wanted was lodged in a barn on the north side of the Hall, one end of which extended into what is provincially called 'a bye-water,' being a branch of the river Wye. The whole quantity consigned to this miserable repository amounted to ten wagon loads. Here the furniture was kept till the moisture arising from floods and rain reduced the woodwork to a state of rottenness and decay; and then it was ordered to be used as fuel." Rayner, who is responsible for the above account, further states that the duke's agent, being short of funds for some requisite repairs to the building, got out of the difficulty by selling such of the *useless lumber* as was not fit for fuel, and that amongst this lumber are known to have been pewter dishes, iron and brass utensils, muskets and swords. Very little of the old furniture now remains at Haddon, but there are some fine pieces of dark oak in the custodian's house, and some oak cabinets and tables found their way to Stanton Woodhouse and Longshawe Lodge, other Derbyshire houses of the Duke of Rutland.

In 1707 Bishop Kennet described Haddon Hall as "a house of no front, no uniform figure, no good avenue on any side, no manner of prospect, no walks or gardens, and, to all appearance, nothing but strength and privacy; no manner of beauty in it." (Restituta, by Sir E. Brydges, Vol. III., p. 362.)

More than half a century later, under date September 1, 1760, Horace Walpole wrote to his friend, George Montagu, "I saw Haddon an abandoned old castle of the Rutlands in a romantic situation, but which never could have composed a tolerable dwelling."

Edward King, however, writing in 1782, seems to have held a somewhat higher appreciation of Haddon Hall. "Much it is to be wished by every lover of antiquities," he says, after giving a quaint description of its parts, that this princely habitation may never come so far into favour, as to be modernized, lest the traces of ancient times and manners, which are now so rarely preserved in this country anywhere, should be utterly lost also here." (Archæologia, Vol. 6.)

His wish has been fulfilled. Haddon Hall has been carefully kept in repair, but never restored, much less modernized. The fifth Duke of Rutland, in receiving the members of the British Archæological Association at Haddon in August, 1851, said, "I think there is no man who holds a possession more proud of that possession than I am of this old Hall," and the same spirit may be said to have animated his successors. The idea of restoring Haddon Hall so as to fit it for a place of residence has been more than once entertained, but always abandoned, as it has been recognised that it would be impossible to live there to-day without making such alterations to the building as would for ever destroy its artistic charm and historic interest. Had Horace Walpole written that Haddon could no longer compose a tolerable dwelling he would simply have been stating a truth. As it was, he only showed how little he understood the life of the Middle Ages. It was because the dwelling was no longer tolerable that the owners finally abandoned it. It was abandoned, however, only as a dwelling. Repairs to the structure are continually going on such as to ensure its preservation, and to render unnecessary any such scheme of restoration as has destroyed the character of so many mediæval buildings.

In 1898 it was found that the north-west entrance tower was nearly eleven inches out of the perpendicular. When excavations were made it was discovered that the whole tower rested on no solid foundation, being built almost from the surface. There were several feet of soil or shale between the base of the tower and the rock, and the wonder is that it had stood for three centuries before beginning to show signs of instability. The intervening space between the base of the tower and the solid rock is now filled with blue bricks of a most enduring description, and all future danger is thus averted. This work was carried out in 1899.

Mention should be made of the visit of Queen Victoria to Haddon Hall in October, 1832. The Princess Victoria, as she then was, came over to

Haddon with her mother, the Duchess of Kent, from Chatsworth, where they were then staying. It is said that "when the royal party visited Haddon in 1832 the tapestry afforded them much gratification and amusement, especially on observing that the various costumes on it exactly corresponded with some of the dresses of the ladies in the royal suite."[1]

Forty years later, in the winter of 1872, King Edward VII. and Queen Alexandra, then Prince and Princess of Wales, visited Haddon, and were entertained at luncheon by the Duke of Rutland in the Great Hall, "when the boar's head and peacock in pride were carried in, and formed part of the fare, as in olden days, while once more musicians filled the minstrels' gallery, great logs blazed in the huge fireplace, and scarlet hangings were spread over the walls."

1 *The Gem of the Peak*, by W. Adam, 1843.

CHAPTER II.—THE EXTERIOR.

For time has softened what was harsh when new,
And now the stains are all of sober hue;
The living stains which Nature's hand alone,
Profuse of life, pours forth upon the stone.

CRABBE.

The nature and position of the site which Haddon Hall occupies has had not a little to do in producing that picturesque effect in its exterior appearance, which is one of its chief characteristics.

Built on a natural platform of limestone rock, which here breaks the somewhat gentle slope of the hillside along the Wye valley, every irregularity and unevenness of the ground has been taken advantage of by the builders of the house, and with the happiest results. The beauty of Haddon lies largely in its happy unconsciousness, its spontaneity, and the excellent fitness of the buildings, which seem to have grown to their purpose rather than to have been worked out as a design.

The platform on which the house stands is far from being level, following pretty nearly the slope of the hillside, but breaking off abruptly on the river side, where it rises steeply from the meadows. This fall in the ground from east to west produces a bewildering difference of floor levels, making an intelligible plan of the building, for general use, very difficult to produce. Haddon Hall has been said to step down, rather than to stand upon, the hillside, and it further seems to have been less built upon, than to have grown out of, its rocky seat.

Roughly speaking, the buildings at Haddon form a parallelogram built round two courts separated from one another by the Great Hall. The whole space covered is about 250 feet in length by 150 feet in width. The longer sides face north and south, the shorter east and west.

The hillside above Haddon is thickly wooded, and, indeed, viewed from the rising ground at the other side of the valley, the Hall appears bosomed in trees. The principal approach in former days was by the old road which descends through the wood from the top of the hill to the gateway under the north-east tower. Little is seen of the building, however, approaching it from this direction till one is close upon it, and the first impression will be one of disappointment.

It is by the more usual way of the modern high road between Bakewell and Rowsley, or by the field paths along the side of the river that the visitor usually approaches Haddon Hall. From either side the first view of the Hall is very striking. On the Bakewell side the trees prevent a good distant view of the building, little but the top of its turrets being visible till one gets close to, when the north-west tower seems to detach itself. The extent of the house is much better seen from the Rowsley side, the view embracing the whole of the beautiful garden front, the chapel, and the western range of buildings, with the turrets and battlements of the two entrance towers rising against a bank of trees. Coming nearer, the rocky nature of the site is at once made evident by the appearance of the western side of the building and of the huge buttressed walls of rough unmortared stones which support the different levels of the gardens.

Being the outcome of something like five centuries of building, we should expect to find the many changes of architectural style strongly expressed at Haddon Hall on the outside of the building. But this is not the case. Haddon Hall preserves a remarkable unity of character in its various parts. The later work harmonizes so well with the old as to produce almost the impression of the house having been designed all at one time, instead of its representing, as we know, the continuous building tradition of many centuries. Mr. Duesbury called attention to the unusually Gothic character of the Elizabethan work, and added: "I suppose the explanation is that the workmen were so accustomed to Gothic treatment and forms of mouldings that they could not leave them off, and were tempted to continue that which they found existing; the battlemented form of parapet was most likely adopted to carry out the harmonious effect of the skyline." There seems to have been an unbroken building tradition at Haddon Hall throughout the days of the Vernons. It is not till the times of the Manners that the Renaissance spirit shows itself at all, and as far as the exterior of the building is concerned it is only manifested in the terrace steps and balustrades in the gardens.

Local workmanship most probably is accountable for the uniformity and simplicity of treatment of the work at Haddon. "The stony soil gave the walls, the local mine the lead roofing, and the broad planks of the floors had needed the destruction of many of its stately trees. Native as was the material, so even more was the workmanship; work lacking the town-made finish, but having the character and honesty of nature's craftsmanship. The outdoor life of the country, the very roughness of the setting, had found an echo in the fabric of the Hall."[1] It would, perhaps, be nearer the truth to say that the several generations of builders and craftsmen, perhaps of the same families, who followed one another at Haddon Hall, having little knowledge of the outside world, got so accustomed to Gothic treatment as to continue unconsciously to build in that style, than that the later builders copied the work of their predecessors deliberately, so as to produce an harmonious effect.

Approaching the Hall from Bakewell, just before turning off the road to cross the bridge, a square stone building is passed on the left, standing by

[1] *An Old House.*—A paper read before the Birmingham Architectural Association, January 24, 1896, by Mr. Arthur T. Bolton.

Geo. Cross, Photo]

THE CUSTODIAN'S COTTAGE AND STABLE.

itself on the high ground of the meadow. This is the old DOVECOTE belonging to Haddon Hall. It is about 23 feet square, and has a two-light window on each side in the upper portion. The door is on the east side away from the road.

The present BRIDGE of three arches across the Wye was built in 1663 by the eighth Earl of Rutland. In the steward's accounts under date of August 10 of that year is this entry:

"Paid to John Milner & Charles Hadfield at severall tymes for makeing the new ston bridge at Haddon, being hyred by the great, wth what my honable Ladie was pleased to give them in all."	97-00-0.

"Hired by the great" means to work by measure, as distinguished from work done by day.

Crossing the bridge the visitor finds himself at the foot of the rock on which Haddon Hall is built. The CUSTODIAN'S COTTAGE and the OLD STABLE stand here, the strong masonry and sturdy buttresses of which latter building should be remarked. In the garden of the cottage are two clipped yew trees fashioned into a boar's head and a peacock, the crests respectively of the families of Vernon and Manners.

The walls of Haddon Hall are largely constructed with small irregular pieces of limestone quarried from the site in the forming of foundations, terraces, and gardens, but a good deal of local sandstone is also used, especially in the bay-windows, chimneys, battlements, and for dressings generally. This sandstone, to which time has given a rich and sober colouring, imparts a warmth to the exterior of Haddon Hall that the cold blue tone of the limestone rubble would be alone unable to produce. Where the limestone is unrelieved the walls look merely cold and severe. The older work is unevenly coursed, and the stones of all manner of sizes, the later work is, generally speaking, built in regular courses with long and thin pieces.

The chimneys, which are very numerous, are mostly square stone shafts crowned with miniature battlements, but here and there are some of a different type, more Elizabethan in character, the battlemented tops having given place to mouldings.

The roofs are low-pitched and lead-covered, and are hidden behind high battlemented parapets. There are numerous ways on to the leads from different parts of the house. The Great Hall has a gabled roof (which was stripped of its old grey slates and covered with blue about fifty years ago), and there are two small gabled roofs over the rooms between the great hall and the kitchen, and another over one of the flanking portions of the north-east tower. Except in these four cases, the gabled roof, generally so conspicuous a feature in mediæval houses, is entirely absent from Haddon Hall.

The North Front, which faces the visitor as he ascends the steep path towards the principal entrance, is rather severe in treatment, but is relieved from monotony by the bold break in the centre, where advantage has been taken of the fall of the ground and of the bold projecting mass of the kitchen chimney to constitute this the chief feature of the grouping of the façade. At each end of the front is a flat-topped battlemented tower with turrets, but so considerable is the fall of the ground that a horizontal line drawn from the ground under the archway of the upper entrance under the north-east tower, would pass at a considerable height over the archway of the lower entrance under the north-west tower. There is, in fact, a difference of about thirty feet between the levels of the ground at these two points.

The uniformity of style that has been referred to as a characteristic of Haddon Hall is, perhaps, nowhere better illustrated than in the north front, where nearly the whole of the elevation is the work of Sir George Vernon, and consequently belongs to the sixteenth century. Its general appearance is the work of a much earlier date. Three or four building periods are, however, represented in the north front, as will be at once apparent when the nature of the walling is examined. The extreme eastern portion, which forms one of the flanking portions of the north-east tower, is part of the fabric of the fourteenth century, and may indeed retain parts of yet older walls. It is built in a rough fashion with irregular pieces of limestone, and the parapet is carried on corbels which have almost the appearance of Norman work. There is a straight joint in the masonry between the north-east tower and the range of rooms adjoining which clearly marks the junction of the sixteenth with the fourteenth century work. The lower portion of the kitchen chimney appears to be earlier in date than the walling on each side and above it. The western end of the front, including the entrance tower and about twenty-five feet of the wall east of it, form the termination of the western range of buildings finished by Sir George Vernon probably before the end of Henry VIII.'s reign. The rest of the north front, which is practically the whole of the line of buildings between the two towers, belongs to the earlier years of the last building period at Haddon. It may have been completed before the garden front, but some portions would probably be in progress at the same time. Yet the contrast between the two is very marked.

The North-West Tower itself is about fifty feet high, with a turret in its south-west angle corbelled from the first floor level. The coats of arms and initials of Sir George Vernon and his first wife might suggest even a later date than that mentioned above, but it may be supposed that Sir George executed the work according to the

Geo. A. May, Photo]

THE KITCHEN CHIMNEY.

plans of Sir Henry Vernon, and merely introduced his own coat of arms and initials to identify himself with the work.[1] But even assigning the north-west entrance tower to the fifth decade of the sixteenth century, the purity of the Gothic style is remarkable. The tower is four storeys in height, the lower, or ground floor, being occupied by the great arched gateway that forms the entrance to the lower courtyard. This is now the principal entrance to the house, but was formerly only intended for those who approached the hall on foot. Mounted guests who did not enter by the principal entrance in the upper courtyard would probably leave their horses at an inn or stable at the bottom of the hill, which, as Edward King puts it, "an horse can hardly climb." There is, however, a mounting block at the top of the hill near to the entrance. Above the gateway the wall is pierced at each storey with a low three-light window with stone mullions and square hood mouldings. The details are simple and even clumsy, but the general effect is very picturesque, the disposition of the windows being very good. Over the doorway and each of the windows immediately above is a square stone panel under a hood mould. The three lower panels have been restored, and two of them are quite plain. That over the first floor window has two plain shields. The upper panel, which is larger than the others, breaks the line of the string

[1] Duesbury.

course under the parapet, and is original. It bears the Vernon crest and helm. The character of the walling of the lower portion of the entrance tower suggests it having been built some years before the upper. The tower terminates with a square battlemented parapet, under which is a moulded string course with grotesque gargoyles. The parapet is constructed, as throughout the building, in local sandstone.

The entrance screen west of the tower, and the two angle buttresses, show a more refined use of ornament than is to be found elsewhere on the exterior of Haddon Hall. The delicate panelling which runs across the front of the screen under the embattled cresting is continued round the two buttresses, where on many shields the alliances of the Vernons are set forth. Each shield forms the centre of a large cusped quatrefoil set in a square panel. Starting from the buttress and proceeding towards the doorway the coats of arms displayed in the panels are as follows:—1. Remains of Vernon (ancient). 2. Pembrugge. 3. Vernon of Harleston; east side of buttress. 4. Camville. 5. Spernore; face of buttress. 6. Pype. 7. Avenel. 8. Remains of Stackpool; west side of buttress. 9. Trussell. 10, 11, 12, 13, obliterated. 14. Vernon quartering Avenel. 15. Vernon quartering Durversall of Spernore. 16. Vernon quartering Stackpool. 17. Vernon quartering Pembrugge. The shield at the other side of the door is obliterated.

Geo. A. May, Photo]

THE ENTRANCE SCREEN.

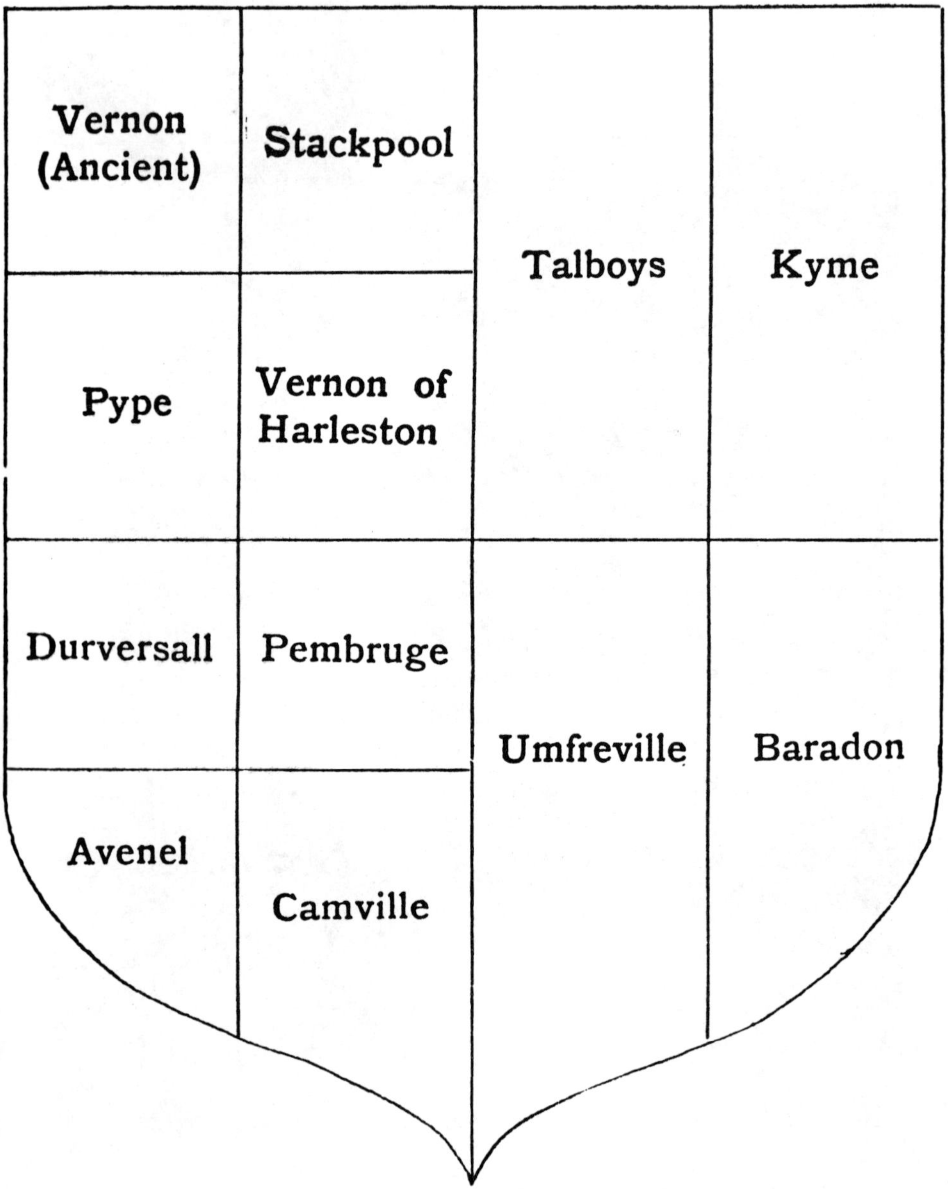

SHIELD ON ENTRANCE SCREEN.

Over the doorway is a great shield of twelve quarterings, Vernon impaling Talboys,[1] with supporters (boar and bull), and the motto above on a scroll "God save the Vernon." On either side of the shield are the initials G.V. and M.V., being those of Sir George Vernon and his first wife, Margaret, daughter of Sir Gilbert Talboys. On the parapet above is carved in high relief the coat of arms of Vernon (ancient) suspended from a crested helm, a fine bit of sculpture.

The kitchen chimney stack is a very clever piece of work, consisting of a complicated series of weatherings, with little windows to light the fireplace, over which a bay-window is formed in the room above by sloping back the angle of the wall. The lower portion of the walling has the appearance, as has been before remarked, of belonging to an earlier building. The masonry is irregular and rough up to the height of the string course; above this it is composed of the regular narrow courses in which nearly all the later work is built. The section of the string courses indicate as well as anything the late date of this northern range of buildings.

Between the kitchen chimney stack and the next break in the wall nearest the entrance tower used

[1] Vernon impaling Talboys. *Vernon*. 1. Vernon (ancient). 2. Stackpool. 3. Pype. 4. Vernon of Harleston. 5. Durversall. 6. Pembrugge. 7. Avenel. 8. Camville impaling Talboys. *Talboys*. 1. Talboys. 2. Kyme. 3. Umfreville. 4. Baradon.

to stand the Brewhouse. The blank wall space and the rougher character of the masonry indicate its position. It was evidently standing when Rayner wrote in 1837, as he speaks of the exterior of the house presenting on the north side "a line almost uninterrupted, except by a square projecting structure with a low roof, supposed to have been a brewhouse." In Lysons' "Derbyshire" (Magna Britannia, vol. 5), published in 1817, a north-west view of Haddon Hall shows this building as a two storey structure with a gabled roof, whose ridge is as high as the battlements of the house. The brewhouse has now entirely disappeared, much to the advantage of the appearance of the north front.

The North-East Tower (known also by the names Eagle, Peverel, and sometimes King John's Tower) is best seen from the east side of the house. The visitor should ascend the steps near the stable, and walk up the hillside along the north front to what was formerly the principal entrance to the mansion. It has been before stated that in all probability the keep of the earliest building at Haddon stood on the site of the north-east tower. The tower proper is immediately over the entrance gateway, and is thus nearly twenty feet back from the angle of the building. The flanking lower portions are, however, apparently of the same or nearly equal date as the tower itself. It is early fourteenth century work, though probably

Geo. A. May, Photo]

THE NORTH-EAST TOWER.

there are a good many stones, and perhaps whole portions of walling, of much earlier date incorporated with it. Mr. Duesbury was of the opinion that the present outer wall is the original wall of a formerly existing castle, built by the first Peverel. He states his case thus:

"The keep [of a former castle] was probably on the site of the north-east tower, and I am inclined to think some of the walls still remain. The corbelling under the parapet looks very Norman, but it cannot be so unless we suppose *all* the doors and windows to have been inserted at a later date. It is evident *some* of the windows have been altered and enlarged, and the eastern arch of the gateway has most probably been rebuilt. It stands more forward than the upper work, and has had large projecting corbels over it to carry a passage of communication round the receding face of the tower above. But this tower is not original, as shown by the corbels on the *inside* of the east wall, over the gateway, in the room on the third storey and level with the external corbels, and proving that at one time this wall was isolated, a mere curtain."[1]

The tower rises to a height of about fifty feet above the ground, and is set back from the face of the wall below, the parapets of the flanking lower portions being broken off at each side.

[1] *Journal of the British Archæological Association*, Vol. vii., 1852.

The passage of communication between these two points would be of timber and has, of course, disappeared. The corbels are at a lower level that those supporting the parapets on either side and have a greater projection. The north-east angle of the tower is chamfered off to the height of about six feet, presumably to allow for a passage way at this side. At the north-west angle is a square watch turret rising about fifteen feet above the leads. This is the highest point of Haddon Hall, and the view from the summit is very fine. The visitor is allowed to ascend the north-east tower, and he is recommended to do so as much for the sake of the interesting bird's-eye view of the building as for the splendid panorama of the surrounding country which is obtained from this point. The battlements are here stepped, not square as in the rest of the building.

The archway under the North-East Tower was formerly the principal entrance to the mansion. It leads to the upper courtyard, round which the state rooms are grouped. There was a road up the hillside communicating with the then only existing road between Rowsley and Bakewell over the top of the hill. This was the only entrance by which horsemen and carriages could enter the Hall.

There is nothing further to be remarked on the Eastern Elevation from this point. This side of

Geo. Cross, Photo]

A CORNER OF THE UPPER GARDEN.

the Hall is cut in two parts by the retaining wall of the terrace garden, which puts a limit to one's steps. The wall is only about six feet above the ground on this side, but there is a considerable drop down on the other side to the level of the terrace. The whole length of the east front, however, as far as the projection of the bay of the Long Gallery, belongs to what has been termed the second building period of Haddon Hall, that is to say, is of fourteenth century date. Plain corbels appear supporting the parapet along the whole length of the front. "Dorothy Vernon's Door," which will be referred to later, was pierced through this older wall. The old corbels may be seen above the door head.

Returning to the north-west entrance we pass through the doorway in the screen and find ourselves opposite the West Front. The return wall of the screen is broken off near to the doorway, but was originally carried some distance along the crest of the hill. The west front presents no remarkable feature. At one end it terminates in the entrance tower at the other in the chapel. The aspect of this side of the house is rather cold and grim, as there are few windows, the rooms being lit from the courtyard. The elevation is best seen as a whole from the river. It is perhaps from this side that the nature of the limestone rock on which Haddon Hall stands, seen rising abruptly from the meadows, is best understood.

The outside wall was originally an enclosing wall and has been twice raised. It had no foundation, and was built on the soil.

The lower portion of the west end of the chapel belongs probably to the earliest building period of Haddon, but the window was inserted in the fourteenth century. The upper part was rebuilt about the beginning of the fifteenth century. The chapel is dealt with at length in the next chapter.

The SOUTH FRONT falls naturally into two main groupings corresponding to the upper and lower courtyards on the inner side. To the right is the Long Gallery, 120 feet in length (outside), with its three great bay-windows. To the left, at a lower level, is the shorter line of the "Earl's Apartments," with three small but beautiful oriels, while the connecting centre space is occupied with the exquisite two-storeyed bay-window which lights the Dining and Drawing Rooms. The garden front is so well known as to need little or no description. It is often described as "the glory of Haddon," and is the favourite aspect of the building for artists and tourists alike. Though gaining much of its beauty from its setting and surroundings, it is nevertheless of very considerable merit when considered simply as an architectural composition. Its beauty is more than that of mere accident. Some portions of the wall of the garden front are undoubtedly very old and belong apparently to the fourteenth century, but as an architectural composition the whole of this façade from the chapel to the terrace may be considered as the work of the latter part of the sixteenth century.

There are but two breaks in the long line of embattled parapets, and these mark the position of the building between the two courts. The effect produced by the series of bays and oriels along the whole length of this front is very striking. With the exception of that to the Dining Room, the bays are all on the first floor, those of the Long Gallery, which are of great size, being carried up from the ground, whilst those of the "Earl's Apartments" next the chapel, are corbelled out. The lower, or ground storey, being occupied by cellars, the windows here are few and of small size. This almost blank lower wall space is largely responsible for the happy effect of the garden front. It gives a strength and a certain severity to the elevation, which would otherwise be lacking, and thus preserves in the latest work that dignity of style which is so characteristic of Haddon Hall, and which may be entirely attributed to the simple treatment of its parts.

The masonry of the south front is much more irregular than that of the northern range of buildings, suggesting that the material of an older wall was employed in its construction. The Dining-Room and Drawing-Room bays are in wrought stone, and over the latter is carved a shield of four quarterings with the Vernon crest and helm.

Between this window and the end of the "Earl's Apartments" will be noticed four corbels similar to those on the east front, about eighteen feet from the ground. This is no doubt part of an original wall that ran along the south side of the house, the upper part of which was removed to make way for later work.

The "Earl's Apartments" were built over a portion of an old curtain wall occupying the space between the chapel and the dining-room, and which now divides the ground storey into two long waste spaces. They occupy the place of a former wooden upper storey, and were practically built round it, the timber framing and roof being still in their place behind the stone walls. The curtain wall still remains, and can be seen from the long narrow apartments on either side of it. The apartment on the garden side has been called the "Aviary," and is longer than the corresponding space on the other side by about half the length of the Dining-Room. There is an entrance from the garden path, and it is worth going in for the sake of examining this old curtain wall, which Mr. Duesbury and others have supposed to be part of the original wall built by Sir Richard Vernon in the days of Richard I., for which he obtained the writ from the Earl of Mortaign previously quoted. Mr. Duesbury writes: "That it was an isolated wall is proved by the fact that there are corbels on both sides of

J. R. Wigfull, Photo]

THE CHAPEL FROM THE UPPER GARDEN.

it; it is about 4 feet 6 inches thick, and above the corbels a foot wider, making it 5 feet 6 inches thick at this point. The increased thickness was doubtless obtained to give space for a passage with a parapet on each side." The corbels are whitewashed over in the room next the garden, and stop where the Dining Room wall begins. They are continued in that portion of the wall which shows outside between the "Earl's Apartments" and the chapel.

The south front is terminated by the chapel, which stands at a slightly different angle. There is nothing remarkable about its outside appearance. The contrast between the narrow pointed single-light windows of the south aisle and the square Perpendicular three-light windows of the chancel is very marked. The south aisle belongs to the oldest part of the building, but the rest of the south side of the chapel is of fifteenth century date.

CHAPTER III.—THE INTERIOR.

I have seen
Old houses, where the men of former time
Have lived and died, so wantonely destroyed
By their descendants, that a place like this,
Preserved with pious care, but not "restored"
By rude, presumptuous hands, nor modernised
To suit convenience, seems a precious thing.
P. G. HAMERTON.

It has been well said that probably nowhere in England can the growth of domestic architecture be better studied than at Haddon Hall. The building is, indeed, almost an epitome of all the styles that prevailed in the domestic buildings of our forefathers from the days of the Conqueror to those of the early Stuarts. Outwardly, as it has been pointed out, the mansion preserves a wonderful unity of effect, but in the interior it is quite otherwise. Almost every room bears the distinctive mark of the life and manners of a different age. It is not necessary here to sketch out the course and current of English life in the Middle Ages. In another place the present writer has done this in a brief manner with special reference to Haddon Hall;[1] but assuming this knowledge on the part of the reader, it will not be difficult, with the plan of the building before one, to understand at once the manner in which Haddon Hall assumed

1 *Architectural and Historical Notes on Haddon Hall.*

the aspect it bears to-day. The successive stages of development, showing the alterations that took place in accommodation and arrangement due to an ever-increasing requirement of manners can all be followed out—the all importance of the Great Hall in the fourteenth century, the addition of the "Dining" and "Drawing" Rooms, when the Lord begins to take his meals away from his dependents, the growing necessity for private chambers of all kinds, culminating in the comparative luxury of the sixteenth century, when the magnificent Long Gallery was built.

The vast number of apartments in Haddon Hall makes it impossible to attempt to give an exhaustive description of every room. To localize many of these apartments, too, would be very difficult, owing to their labyrinthine character, and to the fact of there being no recognised name to describe them by. And, as has been said before, an easily understood plan of the house is very difficult of production.

Even the chief apartments of the house, which are shown to visitors, have names attached to them that cannot in any way be accepted, in all cases, as their correct or original designation. In an interesting series of inventories at Belvoir of the furniture, silver, pewter, linen, and other effects at Haddon Hall, taken at intervals from 1623 to 1730, the names of the rooms occur in the following order:

"The wainscotted parlour. The wainscotted hall. The buttery. The strong beer cellar. The bread house. The wine cellar. The bake-house. The bolting-house. The brew-house. The dairy house, milk-house, and inner-house. The kitchen. The pastry. The inner pastry. The wet-larder. The wash-house or nether dairy. The cellar in the nether court. The chapel. The outward chamber to the best lodging next the chapel leads. The best lodging. The drawing chamber to the great chamber. The great chamber. The still chamber. The gallery. The orange chamber. The green chamber. The uppermost chamber in the Upper Tower. The chamber next below. The next chamber. The chamber next under. The chamber called Oxford Gaol. The partridge chamber. The bake-house chamber. The brew-house chamber. The chamber in the new buildings over my master's chamber. The upper wardrobe. The kitchen chamber. My mistress's chamber. The nursery. The little gallery. My mistress's sweetmeat closet. The chamber next the chapel. Sutton's chamber. The school-house chamber. The little chamber adjoining my mistress's chamber in the nether Tower. The parlour under the rose chamber. The rose chamber. The inner chamber. The hunter's chamber. The inner chamber. The uppermost chamber in the nether Tower. The low wardrobe in the nether court. My master's old chamber in the nether tower. The inner chamber to my master's. Sir Roger's chamber, the chimney piece carved with the arms of the house. The inner chamber to Sir Roger's, wainscotted. The lodge. The parlour under the hunter's chamber. The nether stable and saddle house, Windsor. The ox house. The closet over the great oven."[1]

There is difficulty in locating each one of these apartments, and for the purpose of the present volume it is deemed best to call the rooms by the names by which they are best known. "The designations given by Lysons to the apartments," wrote Llewellynn Jewitt, "are probably correct. From his lists . . . we gather the general inference that the rooms in the west side of the lower court were, in the latter days of its occupation, devoted to the officials of the household; those on the entire south side were the state rooms; those on the east side of the upper court were the family apartments, the bedrooms extending down to the intersection of the lower court; those over the front archway, etc., were the nursery apartments; and the library is believed to have occupied the rooms between, these and the entrance tower." Many of the rooms were probably not arranged on any very definite plan, but put to whatever use that was required.

Entering Haddon Hall by the north-western

1 Carrington. *Journal of the Derbyshire Archæological and Natural History Society*, Vol. xxii.

entrance, under the "nether tower," the visitor is shown all the principal rooms of the house in something like the following order: Lower Courtyard, "Chaplain's Room," Chapel, Kitchen and Offices, Great Hall, Dining Room, Drawing Room, Earl's Bedchamber and adjoining apartments, Long Gallery, Ante-room, State Bedroom. From the last-named room the way leads through what is known as the Archers' Room to the stairs by which the north-east, or upper tower, may be ascended. Returning to the State Bedroom, the visitor leaves the Hall by the ante-room, through "Dorothy Vernon's Door," on to the terrace.

Under the archway of the entrance tower, to the right, is the old Porter's Lodge, with its "peep hole," and on the wall outside is an enormous hoop from an old mash tub.

THE LOWER COURTYARD.

The Lower Courtyard is paved with stone, and is entered from the north-west corner by a "flight of irregular steps just within the gate, in such a manner that it is impossible to have admittance otherwise than on foot." The courtyard is irregular on plan averaging about 100 feet by 70 feet, and follows very nearly the natural slope of the ground. The fall is broken by three steps which extend across its whole length, and which add some dignity to the approach of the Great Hall. The buildings surrounding the courtyard are of

Geo. Cross, Photo]

THE LOWER COURTYARD.

J. R. Wigfull, Photo]

THE CHAPEL TURRET.

different dates. To one's right on entering is the western range of apartments, two storeys high, the work of Sir Henry Vernon in the earlier part of the sixteenth century. The masonry is roughly coursed to the height of the first floor windows, above which it is in regular courses narrowing towards the parapet. The entrance to the chapel is at the end of the western range under a wide archway, the head of which consists of one large stone, shaped like a very low four-centred arch.

The beautiful octagonal bell-turret to the chapel was probably the work of Sir William Vernon, who died in 1467. Each of the eight sides is pierced at the top with a two-light pointed opening with cusped heads. Over this is a moulded string course with gargoyles at the angles, and a battlemented parapet. The turret rises from the floor of the courtyard, and has a raised W carved upon it, probably the initial of Sir William. The date of its erection has been ascribed to about 1455.

The wall of the chapel beyond the turret is probably a little earlier in date, the work of Sir Richard Vernon, who died in 1451. It forms the north wall of the chancel, and is pierced by a three-light window.

The flight of steps adjoining give access to the state apartments without passing through the Great Hall. They are probably of contemporary date with the original half-timber upper rooms east of the chapel, though most likely renewed, and the present parapet walls built, when the "Earl's Apartments" were erected.

To the left of the steps are what are best known as the "Earl's Apartments," built over the old curtain wall referred to in the last chapter. These take the place of a wooden upper storey that formerly existed over the curtain wall, the upright posts of which may be seen in the ground floor room entering from the lower courtyard. The timber framing of the upper portion has been recently exposed in the room above, and may be seen behind the stone wall of the Page's Room. These walls, being very thin, were strengthened by carrying the bay-windows up solid from the ground level. There are two bay-windows to the courtyard, with a chimney between. The chimney is of the later type, and the whole of the walling is constructed with large squared sandstone blocks. These apartments belong to the latest building period at Haddon, and are probably the work of Sir George Vernon.

The east side of the Courtyard is occupied by the Great Hall and its adjoining apartments. This is early fourteenth century work in the main, but the porch and chimney were later additions. The porch is opposite the end of the screens, and is three storeys in height, with a turret at the north-east corner. The entrance is under a pointed archway, above which, on the first floor, is a plain, square-headed, two-light window. Above this on the floor above is a larger two-light traceried window under a rectangular dripstone. The porch has a bold projection, and forms, in reality, a low tower with battlemented parapet. It is divided horizontally by a string course above the first floor window. Under the parapet there are grotesque gargoyles at the angles. There is also a two-light window on the first floor on the southern return of the porch, breaking the string course, with some good tracery in the head. Over the doorway are two shields carved with the arms of Vernon and Pembrugge, which fixes the date of the porch somewhere about 1370, if we assume, as is most likely, that they were put there by the Sir Richard Vernon who married the sister of Sir Fulk de Pembrugge of Tong. The porch is faced with wrought stone in regular courses, but the sides show a rough limestone walling similar to that of the Great Hall. The chimney fills up the whole space between the two windows which light the hall on this side. It is about fourteen feet wide at the bottom, but sets back above in a series of weatherings. It is built with large square stones in irregular courses.

The windows of the Great Hall occupy the full height of the wall under the parapet. They are pointed windows of two lights, divided by a transome, with a trefoiled head to each light and a quatrefoil above.

Before the fireplace was added there were no doubt three windows in this side of the hall, breaking the line of the roof with small gables as at Stokesay, in Shropshire. Later, when the chimney was added, the wall was raised by the addition of a parapet, which is rather clumsily contrived on the chimney stack, and which rather detracts from the beauty of the windows by its heaviness.

The south-east angle of the courtyard shows the junction of the fourteenth with the sixteenth century work. The line of the Great Hall is broken by the projection of the Dining Room, which is lighted from the courtyard by a low eight-light window of great beauty, under a rectangular hood-mould. Above this is a square window of much later date, lighting the Drawing Room, probably inserted in place of an older one. It has five lights, and is divided by two transomes.

The fourteenth century building continues to the left of the porch, and the sixteenth century northern range of apartments abut against it. These have been built out into the courtyard in the north-east corner, so as to gain an entrance from the outside on the level of the principal floor. The junction of this later work with that of the earlier period of Sir George Vernon, will be at once seen on the north side of the courtyard by the straight joint in the walling just where the fall-pipe occurs and by the character of the walling itself.

The view looking towards the entrance tower from the opposite side of the lower courtyard is rather striking, and indicates, perhaps, better than

Geo. Cross, Photo]

ENTRANCE TO LOWER COURTYARD.

Geo. A. May, Photo]

Geo. A. May, Photo]

LEAD RAIN-WATER HEADS IN LOWER COURTYARD.

anywhere else the difficulties that the builders of Haddon had to contend with in the matter of levels. Access is gained to the lower storey of the northern range from the level of the entrance before the first flight of steps is ascended. There is some remarkable corbelling in the angle over the inner archway, in which a good deal of ingenuity is displayed. The space demanded by the main entrance, as well as by two internal spiral stone staircases, rendered the wall at this point somewhat weak, and to bind it securely to the tower this peculiar squinch work was devised.

The lead rain-water pipes in the lower courtyard were probably put up by Sir John Manners (1567-1611). The heads are very handsome, being decorated with pierced panels set against an inner casing. The ears bear the Manners and Vernon crests—the peacock and boar's head.

THE "CHAPLAIN'S ROOM." This is a misnomer, the real Chaplain's Room having been on the first floor, near the chapel and reached by a circular turret stair near the chapel door. This lower room was probably a waiting room. It is panelled in oak and has a three-light window to the courtyard. In it, and in the closet attached to it, are preserved several objects of interest. Amongst these are the rosettes of a pair of fire-dogs, an old matchlock, a buckskin doublet, two pairs of horseman's boots, pistol holsters, a hunting horn, and a set of pewter dishes and plates.

THE CHAPEL.

The Chapel has a bare and neglected look, in strange contrast to that which it must have possessed in the days when it was used for worship. Of its appearance in the days of the Vernons we can only conceive by mentally banishing the pews, pulpit, and other woodwork put in by their successors, and restoring, in our imagination, the ancient rood-loft, the painted walls, and the stained glass in the windows. The Chapel consists of a nave with north and south aisles and a chancel. The chancel and nave are of the same width and under the same roof. The chancel is of unusual size in proportion to the rest of the chapel. The total length of the chapel is forty-nine feet, and of this the chancel absorbs twenty-eight feet. It is about 14 feet 6 inches wide. The south aisle is about twenty-two feet across and nine feet deep, and is separated from the nave by two pointed arches. The north aisle is very shallow, being only about half the depth of the south aisle. Originally both of the aisles would appear to have been of this narrow width, and the chancel would probably be very short. On the enlarging of the south aisle the altar of St. Nicholas would be removed from the chancel and placed against the east wall of the aisle, and a new altar erected in the new chancel. The quoins marking the line of the outer wall of the early south aisle can be seen on the outside of west wall of the chapel.

The dates of the erection of the chapel have already been given, but may be briefly recapitulated here. The original south aisle was Norman work of the twelfth century, but of this only the centre column and the font now remain. The capital of the column has been cut away so as to fit the arches subsequently erected over it. The four lancet windows to this aisle belong to the Early English style of the next century, when the aisle was widened and the present outer wall built. The octagon pillar and arches of the north aisle were erected in the fourteenth century, when the Decorated style of architecture prevailed, and the lower west window would appear to have been inserted at the same time. The chancel, the clerestorey of the nave, and the arches to the south aisle belong to the Perpendicular period, and were probably erected about 1427, which is the date on the east window of the chancel. Dr. Cox thinks that the clerestorey and the square-headed north and south windows of the chancel are later than the chancel itself, probably about the year 1455, when the bell turret was erected, and the reconstruction of the vestibule and the insertion of the present entrance doorway took place.

A good deal of alteration has been carried out at the entrance to the chapel. The turret staircase, which gives access to the western buildings, and which is entered from the chapel porch, entirely blocks up a window in the north aisle which formerly existed to the east of the door.

The roof is of a very low pitch, and like nearly all the roofs at Haddon is covered on the outside with lead. On one of the beams are the initials and date, "G.M., 1624," which would seem to indicate that the present roof was constructed or repaired by Sir George Manners. Sir George is said to have died in 1623, but the roof may have been his work though not completed till after his death. Probably some of the woodwork belonged to an older Perpendicular roof.

That a chapel stood here in the time of the Avenels we know from the agreement between William Avenel and his sons-in-law (circa 1170), wherein "the chapel of S. Nicholas" is mentioned, but if further proof were needed the presence of the Norman column and font would be sufficient evidence. The mouldings of the base and capital of this column indicate the middle of the twelfth century. It was the parish church, as has been before stated, of the vil or town of Nether Haddon, which accounts for it possessing the right of baptism, a right never granted to a mere private household chapel.

The font is round, perfectly plain, and of massive construction, and has a curiously constructed Jacobean wood cover, which, nevertheless, har-

Geo. Cross, Photo]

NORMAN FONT AND PIER IN THE CHAPEL.

monises well with it. It stands close against the Norman pillar of the south aisle, but is not in its original position.

A partial removal of the whitewash from the chapel walls in 1858 led to several discoveries of the former arrangement of the building, and of the coloured decorations of the walls.

By the opening out of a door high up on the north wall the position of the rood loft was determined. The sill of this door is 13 feet 9 inches from the floor of the chapel. This door is reached from the bell turret, the stairs to which start from behind the pulpit, but the ancient rood loft would, however, be in existence before the bell turret was erected. The ends of the pews in the chancel were formed out of the base of the rood screen, which was cut down, and the reading desks inserted, at the beginning of the seventeenth century.

Opposite the door to the rood loft, on the south wall, a curious squint was discovered and opened out at the same time. It is a diagonal opening through the wall, by means of which the altar against the east wall of the south aisle was most probably lighted from a cresset in the thickness of the wall. The niche for the cresset, which would also light the high altar, can be seen from the nave. From the top of the niche a smoke shaft is carried up to the top of the parapet. The squint through which the light shone is in the north-east angle of the aisle immediately above the arch. It can best be seen from the seat nearest the east wall of the south aisle looking up.

There were two altars in the chapel, one in the usual position at the east end, and the other against the east wall of the south aisle. The altar stones yet remain, and may be seen on the floor in the places where the altars formerly stood. That at the east end of the chancel is eight feet long by three feet wide, and is eight inches thick. The edge has a fillet (three inches deep) and chamfer. The surface is decayed, and only one of the consecration crosses is at all distinct. The altar stone in the south aisle is five feet six inches long by two feet six inches wide, and has a fillet and chamfer on the edge. All of the five consecration crosses can be distinctly seen. "This side altar," says Dr. Cox, "was dedicated to S. Nicholas, as we learn from the Chantry Roll of Henry VIII. where the chantry is thus described:—

"Haddon. The service of S. Nicholas in the Chapell att Haddon. The incumbent Sir Rychard Rawson was put in by the executors of Sir Henry Vernon. Clere vj*li*, xij*s*, ij*d*. It hathe a chambre in the manor-place of Haddon by the sufferaunce of Geo. Vernon, Esq. He occupieth a chales and other necessaries of the said George Vernon." "

The altar in the twelfth century chapel at Haddon we know to have been dedicated to St. Nicholas. Later, when the great chancel was added, St. Nicholas' altar seems to have been moved to the south aisle and turned into a chantry altar. The altar at the east end of the chancel was dedicated to St. Michael and St. Anne. Their figures occur in the glass in the north window. In the will of Sir Henry Vernon, proved May 5, 1515, occurs this entry: "Item. I will that there be a priest perpetually singing and there abiding in Nether Haddon according to the will of my grandfather, to serve God, Saint Michael, and St. Anne, and to pray for my soul." Sir Henry's grandfather was the Sir Richard Vernon who built the chancel, and whose name is on the east window.

On the east wall of the south aisle is a bracket in the form of a human head, probably to support the figure of a saint.

There are marks of a large bracket on the north side of the altar in the south aisle, which appears to have been broken off at some subsequent period. Underneath, on a block of stone, are the base mouldings of a detached Early English shaft. It has been suggested that this shaft supported the bracket above, but the stone on which the base mould rests does not appear to be in its original position. Dr. Cox thinks that this fragment is part of a no longer existing thirteenth century arcade.

Against the west wall of the south aisle is a large oak chest, which was probably used for keeping vestments. There are two shields on the panels in front, one bearing the Vernon arms, and the other quarterly 1st Pembrugge, 2nd and 3rd Vernon, 4th Pype. This shows the chest to be of fifteenth century date. The late Duchess of Rutland, quoting from a Journal of the fifth Duke, has stated that "the deeds of the estate were kept in the chapel in a large wooden chest, and during the Civil Wars the rents were deposited after their collection under the chapel floor beneath the seats devoted to the use of the retainers."

Behind the door, to the right on entering the chapel, is a fifteenth century stoup of somewhat unusual size and construction. It stands against the wall, but is detached from it, and has the appearance of a small font. The basin is octagonal with a battlemented rim, and is twelve inches across. The stoup stands on an octagon pillar with moulded plinth.

At the end of the south wall of the chancel, near the altar, is a piscina with a single drain, within an arched recess, or fenestella.

The sill of the adjoining window is very low, to serve as a sedilia.

At each side of the great east window is a bracket for a statue or effigy.

The sloping sill of the east window has been cut away in three places, forming small level spaces presumably for a crucifix and candlesticks.

The windows are not architecturally remarkable,

but the Ancient Glass in the east and north windows is deserving of very careful attention. Of this glass Mr. Jewitt writes: "It gives an excellent example of very good effect produced by very simple means, and excluding very little light from the interior. The drawing, both in expression and in the grace of the drapery, is often very good. Yellow stain is extensively employed, but otherwise colour is sparingly, though very effectively, used. There are no canopies or other architectural accessories. The quarries, forming the groundwork of the windows, come close up to the figures. There are eight patterns of quarries remaining, besides six birds, each of a different form. Most of these patterns are good, and the whole of them may be found in the east window, except one which is in the south-west window of the chancel."

Other windows in the chapel were formerly filled with stained glass, but in 1828 the greater portion of it was taken out and carried off during the night. The offer of a reward of a hundred guineas was made in vain for the discovery of the thieves, and it has been supposed that the glass was conveyed abroad and there sold. The whole of the glass from the lower west window was thus lost, along with a good deal from the windows in the chancel.

The East Window is of five lights under a pointed arch, with thirteen openings in the tracery above. Much of the glass has disappeared, and what remains was releaded in 1858, and arranged as far as possible according to the original design. No new coloured glass was introduced, but some old quarries were collected from other windows of the chapel and placed in the east window. "The original scheme of the glass," writes the Rev. Charles Kerry, "seems to have consisted of a crucifixion in the centre, with SS. Mary and John on either side, each of these being backed by saints in the outer lights. The figure of S. John Baptist seems to have been placed in the room of S. John the disciple, because the figure of the Virgin[1] on the other side occupies the normal position. We may hence safely conclude that the figure of the Evangelist formerly occupied the corresponding position under the cross opposite the Virgin Mother, and that therefore the figure of the beloved disciple was one of the stolen portions. From the pose of the Baptist, turning *towards* the central figure, it is probable that he was originally placed in the *outer* light *on the same side*, and that the fragment of the episcopal figure in the bottom of that outer light was brought here from some other window. There has obviously been an attempt to *balance*

1 Mr. Kerry is probably in error regarding this figure. Mr. H. A. Rye supplies me with the following note: "This figure cannot be Our Lady at the cross, most likely a figure from some other window. Whoever saw Our Lady at the cross with a book in her hand? The upper robe of Our Lady is usually blue, not white. Part of the border is of a totally different pattern to the rest The under kirtle is usually red, not blue. The figure of the Bishop may have been the figure of St. Nicholas and have been over his altar."

the window after the robbery, by glass brought from some other place in the chapel, and this is abundantly proved by the corresponding piece on the opposite side having a *small kneeling* figure at a prayer desk, utterly at variance with the scheme and proportions of the whole window."[1]

All the larger lights of the tracery, with one exception, retain their original single figures in yellow stain. In the uppermost leaf of the trefoil over the centre light has been inserted a shield with the quartered arms of England and France. The colour is obtrusive and out of keeping with the rest of the glass.

Below the three central figures are three shields of arms supported by kneeling angels. The first coat is that of Stackpool, the arms of the mother of Sir Richard Vernon, who erected the window. The second, or central coat, is that of Vernon with a canton. Above the second shield is the inscription on a scroll "Ricardus Vernon milt." The third shield is blank. These shields no doubt formerly occupied the whole breadth of the window, but the lower portions of the outer lights are now filled with fragments representing a knight kneeling at a desk, and an ecclesiastic in eucharistic vestments.

At the bottom of the window, running across the whole of its breadth, the original inscription

1 Derbyshire Archæological and Natural History Society's Journal. Vol. xxii.

yet happily remains. It is in black letter, as follows:

"Orate pro aībus | Ricardi Vernon | et Benedicta uxors | eius que fecerunt anō | dñi Millesimo ccccmo xx.vii. | Istam." |

This inscription never seems to have been carefully looked into. No one has ever given the last word after the date, *istam*, which is out of place. So unfortunately the commemorative inscription is not perfect, but would most likely have been "Orate pro aībus Ricardi | Vernon et Benedicta uxors | eius que fenestram istam | fecerunt ano dni Millesimo ccccmo xx. vii." | If the two unlikely scrolls were removed there would be ample room.

The North Window is of three lights, with six smaller lights in the tracery above under a square head. Of this window Mr. Kerry says: "Of all the ancient painted glass remaining in Derbyshire there is hardly any so perfect as in the north window of the chapel at Haddon. As it is obviously of the same period as the large east window, executed at the period of the highest development of the glass painters art in England, it possesses some of its most charming features. Its admirable preservation is, without doubt, owing to its sheltered position in the south west corner of the courtyard."

The first of the larger lights has the figure of St. Michael with a seven-headed dragon beneath his feet, pierced with his sword. The centre light has a representation of St. Anne teaching the youthful Virgin, and the third light depicts St. George contending with the dragon. The three figures form a band of colouring running across the centre of the window. In the lower part of each light is a shield of arms. The first is that of Trussell.[1] The shield in the second, or centre, light bears the arms of Vernon, with a canton gules (now white), and above is the name Richard Vernon, in black letter. A quarry above the second shield has the Staffordshire knot. The third shield has only some fragments of coloured glass.

Each of the six smaller lights above contains a single figure executed in white glass. According to Mr. Kerry the figures, from left to right, represent St. Matthew, St. Bartholomew, St. James the Great, St. Paul, St. James the Less, and St. Leonard the patron of prisoners and captives.

In the South Window of the chancel are some remains of painted glass with the arms of Vernon impaling a missing coat, and a shield with the arms of Pype. Over the latter is a fragment of the original inscription "Mergareta Pype ux ej."

There are traces of painted glass in some of the other windows in the chapel.

Of the Mural Decorations of the chapel only a

[1] Rayner says in his time (1837) the Trussell arms were in the south window. They have evidently been removed from there to the north. Sir Richard Vernon (d. 1376) married Juliana Pembrugge, heiress to her brother, Sir Fulk de Pembrugge, who married the daughter of Sir William Trussell.

few traces now remain. These were exposed in 1858 on the partial removal of the whitewash, and are of various character. They are described at length by Mr. Jewitt, from whose account the following particulars are taken.

The oldest fragment is a running pattern of good design on the arches of the north arcade, and of the same date as the stonework on which it appears, viz., about 1310. Over the western arches of the nave arcade there are traces of two different designs one on each wall. Both are much defaced. On the west wall of the nave there is a design, consisting of a running pattern of rose branches and leaves, with red flowers of five petals. The stems and leaves are shaded grey and black. The date of this rose pattern is probably about 1427, when the glass of the east window was put in. On the south wall of the chancel is a pattern which enclōsed four groups of figures, two on each side of the window over the sedilia. There is no border surrounding each group, but merely the diaper pattern. They are probably of the same date as the glass of the east window, and are in distemper on the plaster. The figures are black with the exception of some dresses, which are green. There are scrolls to each group corresponding with the number of figures, but without any name. These paintings had been much injured before they were covered with whitewash, and the injury anpears as if partially intentional.

Geo. Cross, Photo]   INTERIOR OF THE CHAPEL.

The groups form a series of subjects, and commence with the upper group on the left (east) side of the window. The subject is the presentation of the Virgin in the Temple by Joachim and Anna. The three figures remain. Below this is a group, much injured, apparently Anna teaching the Virgin to read, whilst Joachim stands by. The upper group on the right (west) of the window is a Holy Family. The Virgin holds the infant Jesus in her arms; St. Joseph stands by; St. John Baptist (?) raises his hands and eyes towards the infant Saviour. Below this is a group, much injured, with four scrolls and apparently four figures. A female figure, probably the Virgin, seems to be carrying a child, whilst a male figure follows behind. There seem to be indications of a fourth and small figure. The subject appears to be the flight into Egypt with, contrary to custom, the figure of St. John introduced.[1]

With the exception of the benches in the south aisle, which are of early date, and the lower front portion of the two chancel pews which are part of the old rood screen, all the WOODWORK in the chapel belongs to the seventeenth century. The exact date when the pews and pulpit were put in cannot be determined, but it is probable that it was shortly after the reconstruction of the roof in 1624. This Jacobean work, which in its own

1 *Haddon Hall*, by Llewellyn Jewitt (*Stately Homes of England*).

way is very effective, consists of two large high pews in the chancel, one on each side, and reaching nearly to the Communion rails. The upper portion of the pews is open and filled in with turned balusters with a cornice moulding on top. At each end, facing west, is a book board supported by a bracket. It is said that the lord and his sons sat in one of these pews and the lady and her daughters in the other. The Manners family were, as we have seen, Protestants, and Nash, in his drawing of the interior of the chapel at Haddon in his "Mansions of England" has given a somewhat puritanic colour to their devotions. In the nave, opposite the first arch of the north arcade, are two long, plain, panelled pews. The pulpit stands at the angle of the chancel and north aisle,[1] and "in such close proximity to one of the pews that had the minister been energetic in his expositions, the lord of the place might have found it best to edge away a little."[2] The pewing and pulpit have stopped mouldings, although the work is much later in date than that in the Dining and Drawing Rooms, where the mouldings mitre all round the panels in the wainscot. The Communion rails and table are apparently of the same date as the pews. The eastern bay of the north aisle is occupied by the organ gallery, which is approached

1 This is not its original position, as it stood against the pillar on the same side.

2 *Haddon Hall*, by J. A. Gotch, 1889.

by a flight of wooden steps near the entrance. It has flat balusters in front. The instrument used is generally supposed to have been a regal, or small portable organ much used during the sixteenth and seventeenth centuries. It was played with the right hand, the left being used to work the bellows. In the steward's accounts for the year 1632 are the following entries:

"P^{d} Ralph Carter for bringing downe the orgaine from London wayeing 18 hundred 21^{li} waight att 8^{s} p 100, & 2^{s} for his man.	007 06 0
"P^{d} Mr. Burwood the Organ Maker his bill of charges for comeing downe wth his man, and in full of the 110^{li} for the Organie, wth 20^{s} to his man.	082 08 0
"P^{d} the Masons for makeing hooles in the chapell to put in the beames of the orgaine flower July 14.	000 04 0
"P^{d} Robt. Tayler his bill for Cutting and squareing timber and makeing seats in the chappell July 21	002 17 8
"P^{d} Maithew Bagshawe for 4 daies worke for the ground worke of the pulpit & makeing the long seate."	000 04 0

These entries seem to fix the date of a portion of the woodwork as 1632, and it is most likely that the chancel pews would be put in about the same time. All this joinery in the chapel is of oak, and was originally painted and gilded. The colour, apparently two very thin coats, has very nearly disappeared. The prevailing tone of colour is now that wonderful silvery grey which old oak sometimes assumes. Traces of the gilding remain. Under date 1640 is an item in the accounts for "painting and guilding the Chappell."

In an inventory of furniture at Haddon in 1637-8, the contents of the chapel are given as follows:

> "The orgaine.
>
> The Communion table.
>
> The carpett of stript stuffe.
>
> A large cushion for the pullpitt of needlewarke lyned with blew norwidg stuffe
>
> 12 brasse candlesticks.
>
> 1 Round bassock.
>
> Psalters.
>
> Bybles."

In the north wall of the chancel near the east window is a black marble tablet which formerly was part of the monument to Dorothy Vernon and her husband in Bakewell Church. When the monument was renovated the inscription on the pedestal between the two kneeling figures was renewed and the original tablet was removed, its place being filled with a new one on which the lettering is more easy to read. After a narrow escape from being taken to America, it was secured by the Duke of Rutland and placed in its present position. The inscription runs: "Here lyeth S[r] John Manners, of Haddon, Knight, second sonne of Thoas, Erle of Rutland, who dyed the 4 of June, 1611. And Dorothie his wife, one of the daughters and heires to S[r] George Vernon, of Haddon, Knight, who deceased the 24 day of June, in the 26 yere of the raigne of Queen Elizabeth, 1584."

The chapel of Haddon is said not to have possessed the rights of sepulture, but as late as the middle of the seventeenth century a burial vault was ordered to be made there by Lady Rutland (wife of the eighth earl), for her three infant children who were buried at Bakewell. She wanted their bones to be removed. This was, however, never done, and in 1841, when Bakewell Church was restored, three small lead coffins were found in the position where the bodies were said to have been buried.

From the chapel the visitor passes across the courtyard to the Great Hall.

THE GREAT HALL.

THE PORCH to the Great Hall has a stone seat on each side. On that to the left is the Roman altar mentioned on page 4. It was dug up between Haddon and Bakewell.[1] It is of common

1 Lysons and Bateman say "in the grounds of Haddon Hall."

Derbyshire sandstone, and stands three feet high. The inscription is much defaced and difficult to decipher, but is thus given by Lysons:

DEO
MARTI
BRACIACÆ
OS[I]TIVS
CAECILIA[NVS]
PRAEF COH
I AQVITANO
V S

The brackets are added to complete the words which are in parts quite worn away. The inscription has been rendered thus: "To the god Mars, Braciaca, Ositius Caecilianus, Prefect of the first cohort of the Aquitani, in performance of a vow." Some antiquaries have considered Braciacae to refer to the name of a place, others have thought it to be an epithet of Mars.

It is from the Great Hall that one can perhaps best realise the appearance of Haddon Hall in mediæval times. Although the roof is not the original, and a side gallery put in by the Manners somewhat disfigures the hall and apparently reduces it in size, this apartment retains far more of the characteristics of the domestic architecture of the Middle Ages than any other room in the house. It was, of course, the common eating room before the

Geo. A. May, Photo]

ROMAN ALTAR.

Geo. Cross, Photo]

THE GREAT HALL.

time when the lords of Haddon began to take their meals in private. There is the raised dais, the screen, and the minstrels' gallery. The fireplace is rather later than the hall itself, the fire having no doubt been originally in a brazier in the centre of the floor, the smoke rising and finding its way out through a louvre in the roof.

The Great Hall is thirty-five feet long by twenty-five feet wide. The floor is flagged and at the upper end is very slightly raised, so as to form the dais. The original table still stands here, one of the finest examples of its kind yet remaining anywhere in England.[1] It is very much worm-eaten and decayed. At the lower end of the hall are the screens, the passage behind which communicates at either end with the lower and upper courts. Over this passage is the minstrels' gallery, access to which was originally gained only from the room over the porch.

The screen and the front of the minstrels' gallery is in oak, and is the only considerable example at Haddon Hall of real mediæval woodwork. It is beautifully panelled, each panel being headed with cinquefoil cusping, with Gothic tracery patterns above of different designs. It is decorated with stags' antlers. The screen has the usual two openings to the passage. Affixed to the screen immediately to the right on entering is a curious kind of fetter lock fitting upon a staple, and so

[1] Jewitt.

fashioned as to secure a man's hand when it became necessary to enforce the laws of conviviality by some form of punishment. Tradition has it that in those days if a man should fail to drink his quota of liquor he was fastened up by the wrist to this ring and the liquor poured down his sleeve, or if guilty of any other breach of the law of decorum of the board, he was similarly secured and compelled to remain during the carousal, being treated now and then not only with a stream of cold water poured down his sleeve, but with other indignities which were forced upon him.

The walls of the Great Hall are panelled in oak to the height of the gallery, above which they are plastered. The panels are square framed, and the work is evidently of the same date as the side gallery, which was erected by the Manners in the seventeenth century to form a passage way between the Drawing Room and the northern apartments of the house. It is much narrower than the minstrels' gallery, and runs along the whole of the east side of the room. The difference in construction between the wood panelling of the Gothic period and that of the seventeenth century is well illustrated in the Great Hall where the screen abuts the later wainscot.

There are two windows to the lower courtyard and one to the upper. They have had recessed window seats. The high pitched roof of the hall is modern and incongruous, and the window over the dais is, of course, a modern insertion.

Geo. A. May, Photo]

"THE WRISTLET."

There are a few pieces of furniture left in the Great Hall at the end of the screen, and about a dozen pictures of no particular merit are on the walls.

Under the window to the right of the fireplace is an old stone quern, or hand mill for grinding corn. It formerly stood in the lower courtyard, where it served as a receptacle for water from a down spout. "The indentations or narrow channels radiating from the centre are perceptible, though very much worn; the metal pivot on which the upper stone resolved has been broken off."[1]

The position of the kitchen and offices in relation to the Great Hall shows that they are co-eval with it though a good deal of re-construction and re-building in the northern part of the house has left them with very little semblance of their original condition. They occupy the position in which such apartments are usually found in mediæval houses. "At the lower end of the Hall behind the screen there were usually three doorways," says Parker,[2] "one to the pantry, one to the buttery, and the central one to a passage between these two apartments leading to the kitchen." This is the exact position at Haddon, but there is, in addition, a fourth door, a later insertion giving access to the rooms above by a new staircase which took the

1 Cokayne.

2 *Domestic Architecture of the Middle Ages.*

place of an outer stair and entrance, traces of which can be seen in the lower courtyard. The space behind the screen was the servants' part of the Hall where a great deal of work had to be carried on.

The four openings behind the screen have each a pointed arch. The first of these near the entrance from the lower court has an oak door with a wicket in the middle, just large enough to pass out a cup or trencher. This room was evidently the buttery, and may also have served as a pantry. There is the ancient oak bread box, the top rail well worn with cutting; there are also the crooks for the hinges of the low half door and the jambs cut away to its height. This would be used in the day time when the hall was in use. From it a flight of steps conducts to a large room or cellar of irregular shape with stone vaulting supported by a central pillar, manifestly designed for a beer cellar. Around the walls are remains of a low stone bench, and on the floor is a drain to carry away drippings. A door from this cellar led to the brewhouse, now destroyed.

The second opening leads to the kitchen, the third to a small vaulted room, supposed to have been a wine cellar, "which," says Edward King, "according to the frugality and ideas of early times, when wine was considered merely as a cordial and dram, needed to be but small." The buttery was probably for the storing and dispensing of

J. R. Wigfull, Photo]

THE KITCHEN CHIMNEY.

beer and malt liquors only. The fourth door leads to a staircase, which gives access to the northern apartments.

The passage to the kitchen is paved with stone, and has a continuous descent. Near its lower end is a gate, the top of which forms a broad shelf. "To this point were the servants permitted to come, but were forbidden access to the kitchen itself. The dishes were placed on the door shelf by the cooks on the one side, and removed by the servitors on the other, and by them carried up the passage to the banqueting hall."[1]

THE KITCHEN.

The Kitchen is of great size, but very low and dark. It measures about twenty-eight feet by twenty-four. The ceiling is carried by massive beams and by a central support of solid oak, and is of late insertion. The height to the underside of the beam is eleven feet three inches. There are two fireplace openings, each thirteen feet across. "The lower part of the kitchen," says Parker,[2] "is perfect, but an upper room has been introduced in Elizabethan work." This is very probable, the view being strongly supported by the appearance of the masonry outside. It would, perhaps, be nearer the truth to

1 Jewitt.

2 *Domestic Architecture of the Middle Ages*, Vol. iii, Part 2, p. 221.

say that the upper walls of the kitchen were removed when the upper chamber was added. At any rate we may be sure that the mediæval kitchen was more lofty and more light than the present apartment. The kitchen was probably originally more detached from the Great Hall than at present. The passage from the screens runs for about twenty-three feet between thick stone walls, after which there is a space on each side from which it is divided by wooden partitions. There are buttresses on the returns of these passage walls, showing that it was originally an outside wall between the Great Hall and Kitchen. In the Kitchen can still be seen the old dressers, stone water troughs, chopping block, and various utensils. The dressers are of solid oak, six or seven inches thick. In one place they are hollowed out into circular basins, one of which is worn through from constant use. There are iron rings in the floor in places by which stones were lifted up to give entrance to drains.

Adjoining the kitchen are numerous larders, store rooms, and pantries belonging to it.

It has been said that Sir George Vernon was noted for his hospitality and "kind reception of all good men." The appearance of the kitchen and offices even to-day gives some indication of the nature of this hospitality. The nature of a large number of entries in the Steward's accounts helps one still more to understand the extent and nature of the work in the kitchen department, not only in the days of Sir George Vernon, but well into the seventeenth century. Between the years 1660 and 1670 there were generally killed at Haddon every year "between 30 & 40 Beefs, & betw[n] 4 & 500 sheep, & 8 or 10 swine." And this was at a time when the family spent most of their time at Belvoir.

THE DINING ROOM.

DINING ROOM. This apartment, originally, no doubt, the Solar, or lord's chamber, is situated at the upper end of the Great Hall behind the dais, from which it was entered through a door no longer existing. The room is now gained from a passage leading from the end of the Great Hall to the garden. This passage was, no doubt, taken off the end of the original apartment, at the time it was made to assume its present appearance. Entering the Dining Room from the Great Hall the contrast is very striking. We are apparently transported at a step from the rough mediæval days when the custom of dining in the hall was still the fashion, to the more refined times of Henry VIII. and Elizabeth. "By the end of the sixteenth century," says Mr. Reginald Blomfield, "the idea of the hall as a common living place was going out of fashion. It was used for Christmas revels and great entertainments, but the master and mistress had their private dining room, and even as early as 1460 a "privy parlour" was attached to the hall at Wanswell Court in Gloucestershire."[1]

The Dining Room at Haddon is a most interesting apartment and very characteristic of its period. It was fitted up by Sir George Vernon, apparently about 1545, which date appears on the panelling. It is a low room, thirty-two feet long by nearly sixteen feet wide. The whole of the walls are panelled in oak as high as the ceiling, which gives it a somewhat sombre appearance not shared by the other state rooms. The end of the room opposite the door is entirely filled with a Gothic window of eight lights, with cusped heads, which looks on to the lower courtyard. The glass of this window is disposed in an elaborate geometric pattern, and in some of the lights are shields in painted glass bearing the arms quarterly of Vernon (ancient), Avenel, Camville, Talbot, Pembrugge, Pype, etc., Vernon ancient, and Vernon impaling Talbot (nearly obliterated).

On the left of the doorway, down three steps, is a deeply recessed oriel window twelve feet deep by seven feet six inches wide, divided into six lights by thick stone mullions. This window, which is very happily placed, looks on to the upper garden, and is clearly a later addition to the room.

The Dining Room ceiling is divided in bays by five beams, the mouldings of which were ornamen-

1 *A History of Renaissance Architecture in England*, i., 78.

Geo. A. May, Photo]

THE DINING ROOM.

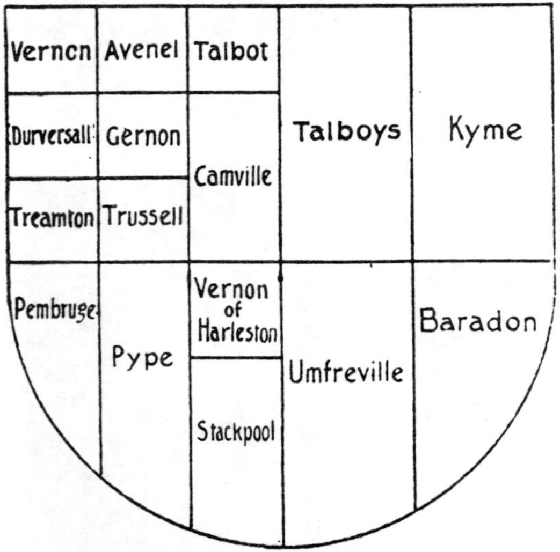

OVER FIREPLACE.

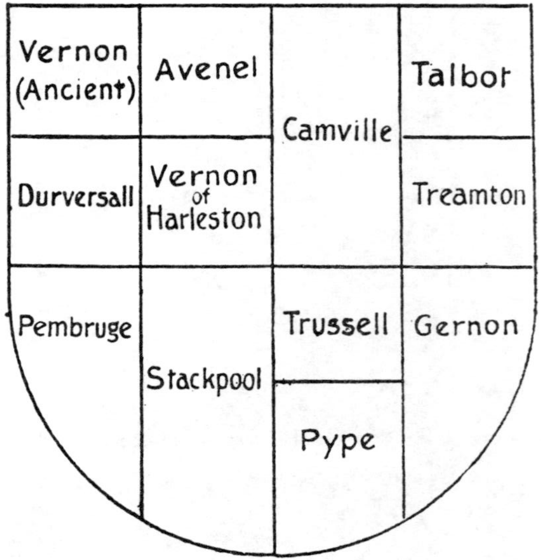

OPPOSITE FIREPLACE.

SHIELDS IN DINING ROOM.

ted with painting and gilding, some trace of which is perceptible. The ceiling was originally coloured and heraldically ornamented. The chipping away of the plaster and whitewash has partially revealed this ancient decoration, which appears to have included the Talbot dog, the Tudor rose, and the ancient coat of Vernon. This is most likely the work of Sir Henry Vernon (1467-1515), who married Anne, daughter of John Talbot, Earl of Shrewsbury.

The Wainscot in the Dining Room, which, as in all other parts of Haddon Hall, is of oak throughout, is particularly rich in decoration. The ornament, however, being concentrated over the fireplace, in the oriel recess and in a kind of frieze along the top of the walls, allows the eye to rest on the plain narrow upright panels of which the wainscot is composed. A very simple moulding mitres all round the panels. The mouldings are worked on the solid, that is, the actual framework of the panel is moulded. Mouldings thus mitred on the solid had almost entirely replaced the older form of stopped mouldings by the end of the sixteenth century, although, as we have seen, stopped mouldings are used nearly a century later at Haddon in the chapel. The larger top panels forming the ornamental frieze extend over three of the panels beneath, and are three feet nine inches long by a foot deep. They contain a succession of shields of arms, which, with one or two exceptions, are placed between boars' heads facing each other and enclosed in circles of various quaint designs. The frieze also contains some smaller panels carved with linen patterns, lover's knots, and other devices.

Turning to the left on entering the room the panels and shields of arms are as follows:

East (or door) side:

Treamton (a bend engrailed).
Gernon (three piles wavy).
Trussell (trellis clouée).

In window recess, east side:

Square panel with boar's head.
Pype (two pipes between nine crosses croslet), impaling Baradon.
Pembrugge (barry of six) impaling Umfreville (a cinquefoil between nine crosses).
A warrior's head within a circle.[1]

Window recess, west side:

Vernon of Harleston (fretty with a canton), impaling Kyme (a chevron between ten crosses croslet): a long panel with the initials G. V. outside the boars' heads.

1 This head is often said to represent Will Somers, court fool, or jester, to Kings Henry VII. and Henry VIII., but there seems to be no reason for the statement. The head is a common Renaissance type. A portrait of Will Somers at Hampton Court shows him a beardless man, quite different in appearance to the so-called 'jester' of Haddon.

Geo. A. May, Photo]

DETAIL OF PANELLING IN DINING ROOM.

PANELLING OVER THE FIREPLACE IN DINING ROOM.

Spernore (three falcons with wings expanded each standing on a staff couped and raguled): a long panel, on either end of which is an elaborate interlacing pattern.

South (or fireplace) side:

Vernon (ancient) impaling Talboys (a saltire and on a chief three escallops) with supporters, a boar and an ox on either side of which are the initials G. V. and M. V. with the words "Ano. Dmi. 1545. Monseigneur de Vernon." The initials are those of Sir George Vernon and Margaret, his first wife, daughter of Sir Gilbert Talboys.

Small shield with the three feathers of the Prince of Wales, and the initials E. P.

The Royal Arms of England (quarterly France and England) with supporters, a greyhound and a griffin.

Quartered shield of Vernon impaling Talboys with quarterings, viz., *Vernon*: (1) Vernon, (2) Avenel, (3) Talbot, (4) Durversall, (5) Gernon, (6) Treamton, (7) Trussell, (8) Camville, (9) Pembrugge, (10) Pype, (11) Vernon of Harleston, and (12) Stackpool. *Talboys*: (1) Talboys, (2) Kyme, (3) Umfreville, (4) Baradon. With supporters, a lion and a boar.

A shield quarterly of four: 1st and 4th three escallops, one and two, 2nd and 3rd chequy (Palmer quartering Warren?)

Stackpool.

A long floriated panel.

North side. Opposite fireplace. Left to right:

Vernon.

Vernon of Harleston.

Pembrugge.

A shield of twelve quarterings of Vernon, namely, (1) Vernon, (2) Avenel, (3) Durversall, (4) Vernon of Harleston, (5) Pembrugge (6) Stackpool, (7) Camville, (8) Talbot, (9) Treamton, (10) Trussell, (11) Pype, (12) Gernon. On each side of this shield is a boar within a circle.

Pype.

Vernon impaling Treamton.

Vernon impaling Talbot.

Avenel.

Over the door in the Dining Room is a Gothic panel about three feet long, with three quatrefoils with roses in the centre, divided by tracery. It is not in its original position, and was most likely brought here from some other part of the house, perhaps the chapel. Indeed, the arrangement of the panelling of the room generally looks as if it had been patched and altered at different times.

Geo. A. May, Photo]

DETAIL OF PANELLING IN DINING ROOM.

Under the royal arms over the fireplace is the motto, taken from an edition of the Bible older than the Authorised Version, "Drede God and Honor the Kyng."[1]

In the oriel recess, in addition to the coats-of-arms and crests, are two panels with the heads of a man and woman, said to represent, but with no sufficient authority, Henry VII. and his Queen, Elizabeth of York. These are immediately over a door which opens on to a kind of cupboard in the wall, but which formerly gave access to the garden. The figures have nothing regal about them, and are of the period Henry VIII., and more likely to be Sir George Vernon and his first wife. The figure and dress of the man are much like Sir George on the tomb of his father in Tong Church.

The panelling throughout the room is surmounted by a carved cornice, but in the oriel recess this cornice is crowned by another of a different pattern, apparently of an earlier date, and not in its original position. That this is not the original decoration of the window is shown by the presence of the rough stone cornice behind. The slope behind the pendant cinquefoils is occasioned by there being a board upon the surface of the stone cornice. The panelling of the east end of the room has been brought forward to form the garden entrance. The original wind porch round the door from the Great Hall to the Dining Room may be traced on the floor.

[1] I Peter ii., 17

The fireplace and grate are curious and interesting, and an old bronze wine cooler in the window at the end of the room merits attention.

From the upper end of the Great Hall, near the entrance to the Dining Room, a stone STAIRCASE leads to the upper floor where the state apartments proper are situated. This Staircase is of Elizabethan date, and the low balustraded door, or dog-gates, beside the use which this name suggests, served as a line of demarcation between the more private parts of the house, and the Great Hall, which gradually came to be used more as a means of communication between the different parts of the house than as a place in which the household lived. In other words, it began to assume something of the nature of the hall in a modern mansion. There is no grand staircase at Haddon Hall, such as we should expect to find if the house were entirely Elizabethan. This modest flight of stone steps is the principal staircase of the house, but not, of course, the only one. The remains of the pullies and staples for causing the gates to be self-closing by means of a weight are to be seen. At the top of the stairs is a landing from which doors lead to the Drawing Room, the Long Gallery, and to a staircase to the leads. On the landing are four pictures, said to represent the Reproof of Peter, The Offering Up of Isaac, Time Destroying her Children, and Princes Rupert and Eugène.

J. R. Wigfull, Photo]

STAIRCASE FROM GREAT HALL.

THE DRAWING ROOM.

THE DRAWING ROOM is immediately over the Dining Room, but is larger than the latter apartment by the width of the passage from the Great Hall to the garden. It is forty feet long by fifteen feet wide, with a window recess in the same position as that in the Dining Room, measuring twelve feet by seven feet six inches. The name is, of course, modern, and it is rather difficult to know exactly what purpose this room served. It has some of the characteristics of the Dining Room, but is higher, lighter, and more cheerful in appearance. Its walls, except in the oriel recess and round the fireplace, are hung with tapestry. The whole of the end of the room is taken up with a large window of five lights divided by two transomes.

Along the top of the walls on three sides of the room runs a deep plaster frieze in five heights, each decorated with a different running pattern of flowers, fruit, etc. This frieze is now, unhappily, whitewashed. It stops at each side of the great west window, round the head of which is a plaster moulding down to the height of the tapestry. The frieze on the wall opposite the fireplace was cut through when the roof of the Great Hall was repaired about fifty years ago, and the ornamental plasterwork destroyed. It is now quite plain.

The panelling in the oriel recess and over the fireplace is more delicate in its details than that in the Dining Room, but, like it, all the mouldings are worked on the solid and mitred. It has been originally painted green and gold, traces of which still remain. The mullions of the bay-window have apparently been cut away for the sake of the view, which from this window is very lovely. The ceiling of the oriel is ornamented with plaster ribs in the form of an eight-pointed star, with intersecting segments of circles attaching the inner angles to one another, and forming a geometric pattern of great beauty.

Opposite the bay-window, behind the tapestry, and up four steps in the thickness of the wall is a doorway which opens upon the side gallery of the Great Hall, already mentioned as having been erected in later times in order to connect the upper rooms of the two sides of the house.

The copper fire-dogs in the Drawing Room are very fine. They have each two circular bosses of open metal work of the most chaste and elaborate design and workmanship. There is also a curious old grate in the fireplace with alternate upright bars terminating in fleurs-de-lys.

The tapestry in this and other rooms is described at length by Lady Victoria Manners in her *Descriptive Notes on the Tapestry in Haddon Hall*. There are five pieces of Flemish manufacture. The subjects are all woodland scenes, with borders composed of fruit, flowers, and medallions, the colouring being of a bluish green.

Geo. Cross, Photo.

THE DRAWING ROOM.

The old iron hooks for holding back the tapestry from the doors when so required still remain.

Two round oak tables and four upholstered settees are preserved in this room.

THE EARL'S APARTMENTS.

From the lower end of the Drawing Room a door leads to the suite of rooms generally known as the Earl's Apartments. These were erected at a later date, and are three in number, the central, or largest, being known as the Earl's Bedchamber. Before this and entering immediately from the Drawing Room is an ante-room, sometimes called the Earl's Dressing-room, and beyond it is the Page's Room, sometimes called—but without good reason—the Lady's Dressing-room. These rooms are hung with tapestry, and belong to the last building period at Haddon. The name "Earl's Apartments" is given to them, as they were used by the Earls of Rutland when visiting Haddon. The earldom of Rutland came to the Haddon Manners in 1641, when John Manners, grandson of Dorothy Vernon's husband, became eighth earl. His son, the ninth earl, was created Duke of Rutland by Queen Anne in 1703.

The Ante-Room, or Earl's Dressing-room, is a small but remarkably pretty apartment lighted by a single bay-window to the garden. From the fireplace in this room it is said that Count Rumford

(Benjamin Thompson) obtained his plan for preventing smoky chimneys. The walls are hung with tapestry. Over the mantelpiece is a piece from the series of the "Life of Alexander," representing Alexander receiving the wife of Darius after the battle of Issus. The borders at top and bottom are lacking. In the corner between the window and the door to the Earl's Bedchamber is a hawking scene, and on the north wall is a nearly perfect piece of verdure tapestry.

The Earl's Bedchamber is about twenty-three feet long by twelve feet wide. It is lit by two bay-windows panelled in oak, opposite each other and looking on to the garden and lower courtyard respectively. The walls are entirely hung with tapestry. On the right of the window overlooking the garden is an interesting, but mutilated, piece representing a hawking scene. To the right of the door leading to the Page's Room is a large piece, "The Stag Hunt," with border on top and left side. To the left of the window overlooking the Courtyard is a fragment (temporarily hung) from the Life of Alexander. The east side of the room has, to the right of the door, a fragment representing the entry of Alexander into a city, and on the left a female figure.

The Page's Room is a small apartment fourteen feet by twelve, lit by two bay-windows placed similarly to those in the Earl's Bed-chamber. From this room a doorway opens out to the top of the flight of steps which give access to these apartments from the lower courtyard. A smaller door gives on to a narrow flight of steps leading to the roof of the chapel. Over the fireplace—which is of rather peculiar construction—is an interesting piece of verdure tapestry, which has been pieced together from the fragments left over when repairing a piece, most likely a hanging for the back of the dais in the Hall, having five shields of the Royal Arms of England (now at Belvoir Castle). It is of Flemish manufacture, early sixteenth century.[1]

This series of rooms, as before mentioned, is built over the curtain wall, and is of curious construction. At first the work was of oak timber filled in with plaster and bracketed out from the wall on each side. On the Courtyard side in the Page's Room this can still be seen. At a later date this was faced up from the ground with a fourteen-inch ashlar wall on the Courtyard side, but a more substantial one towards the garden, on which side nearly all the half-timber work has been removed. The fourteen-inch wall beginning to fail and move outwards at the top, the two large bay-windows were erected in the Courtyard to act as buttresses and stay the movement. At the same time the roof was lifted up bodily two feet and ceiled on the underside, covering the moulded spars and timbers.

1 Lady Victoria Manners.

THE LONG GALLERY.

At the head of the staircase from the Great Hall to an ascent on the left by six steps to the entrance of the Long Gallery. Four of these steps are semi-circular on plan, and are of solid oak, said to have been cut from the root of a single tree that grew in the park at Haddon. The Long Gallery is an apartment peculiar to the Elizabethan house, the purpose of which has never been fully explained. "The original idea," says Mr. Reginald Blomfield, "must have been little more than an enclosed walk for bad weather. It is probable that the gallery was suggested by the long, covered passage devised for internal communication between the various parts of the house." It corresponds to some extent to the loggia of the Italian house, and may indeed owe something to Italian influence. The climate of England would not permit of a gallery open to the air as in Italy, but the Long Gallery is generally sunny and light, and with easy access to the garden.

The Long Gallery at Haddon Hall appears to have been built by Sir George Vernon over some earlier rooms. The roof, now hidden by the plaster ceiling subsequently erected, is of early sixteenth century type, with moulded spars, rafters, and purlins, all showing traces of colour. After his marriage with Dorothy Vernon John Manners panelled the room and put up the present ceiling,

Geo. A. May, Photo]

THE LONG GALLERY.

leaving the room pretty much as we see it to-day. The Gallery is 110 feet 6 inches long by 17 feet 4 inches wide. The height is 15 feet. These dimensions, though giving a noble room, do not place this apartment among the number of larger galleries of this period in England. For the sake of comparison the dimensions of some of the best known of these may be stated.

	Length in feet.	Width.	Height
Audley End (destroyed)	226	32	24
Bolsover, 1629 (destroyed)	220	—	—
Hampton Court (destroyed)	180	25	—
Montacute (Somerset)	170	20½	—
Hardwick (1590-7)	166	22½	26
Parham (Sussex)	160	18	13
Aston Hall, Birmingham...	140	18	16
Charlton (Wilts.)	130	22	—
Haddon	110½	17	15

On the south side of the room are three bay-windows overlooking the garden, the centre one being deeply recessed and square on plan, measuring 15 feet by 11 feet 6 inches, large enough for a fair-sized apartment. The end of the room is entirely taken up with a stone mullioned window of eight lights divided by two transomes, and with a window on the north and south walls at each side. On the north side are two windows overlooking the upper courtyard, and between them, and immediately opposite the central bay, is the fireplace. All these windows, with the exception of the great bay, are glazed with diamond-shaped quarries. Those to the great bay are square.

On the first window to the right on entering are the quartered arms of the Earl of Rutland, impaling Vernon, with the date 1589. In the third window are the arms of the Earls of Shrewsbury and Rutland, each encircled by the garter and surmounted by an earl's coronet, and having respectively G. S. and E. R. in the field.[1] In the fourth window are the Royal Arms of England surrounded with the garter, and surmounted by a crown.

The timber for the floor of the Long Gallery is said to have been provided by the trunk and arms of the same tree from whose root the circular steps were cut. The floorboards vary in width from twelve to twenty-two inches.

This apartment has formerly been richly painted and decorated, and must have presented a magnificent appearance in the seventeenth century. The ceiling is now, unfortunately, whitewashed, and the wainscotting, though it has assumed a silvery grey tone which in itself is very delightful, gives one in no way a correct idea of the original decorative treatment of the room, which now looks bare and neglected.

1 George, sixth Earl of Shrewsbury, married as his first wife Gertrude, daughter of Thomas Manners, Earl of Rutland; his second wife was Elizabeth Hardwick, the celebrated "Bess of Hardwick."

J. R. Wigfull, Photo]

PART OF THE CEILING IN THE LONG GALLERY.

The ceiling is slightly coved and relieved by shallow projecting plaster ribs disposed in the form of squares, lozenges, and quatrefoils foliated at their points. The square panels enclose a shield surrounded by a delicate strap-work border and bearing the arms of Manners impaling Vernon. The ceiling was, of course, originally painted and gilded in a very rich manner, traces of which, says Dr. Cox, were, in 1875, "quite obvious and beyond dispute."

The walls of the Long Gallery are wainscotted throughout in oak in a most elaborate manner. The wainscot is entirely different in character from that of the other rooms previously noticed, the details showing that the influence of the Renaissance reached Haddon with the Manners family, whose coat-of-arms first appears in this room. The wainscot is thus described by Mr. Jewitt: "The general design is a series of semi-circular arches, alternately large and small, divided by pilasters with foliated capitals, and surmounted by a frieze and a turreted and battlemented cornice. The pilasters, divided like the whole design up to the frieze, are of three heights. The basement of the wainscotting about one-eighth of its entire height, is plainly panelled, and devoid of all ornament. The second height, rising to more than a third of the whole, is of a much more decorated character. The pilasters are fluted,[1] and

[1] The alternate hollows are filled in with strips of rosewood.

the spaces between them filled in with geometric patterns, the narrower spaces being by far the most elaborate in their design. The third height is a series of semi-circular arches, alternately wide and narrow, divided by the pilasters, the crown of the arch of the narrower ones being on a level with the springing of the larger ones. The whole of the arches, in which pictures formerly hung, spring from small brackets and semi-pilasters at the sides of the pilasters, and are elaborately decorated. Over each of the smaller arches is a shield of the arms of Manners, with a crescent for difference, and surmounted on the frieze by their crest, a peacock displayed, also differenced with a crescent, alternating with the arms of Vernon and their crest, a boar's head. The pilasters in this height are carved in scale pattern, and are finished with capitals of foliage filling up the spandrels of the arches. Above these is the frieze, the spaces of which are occupied respectively with the crests just named, alternating with the rose and thistle conjoined on one stem.[1] Above this is a remarkably fine turreted and battlemented cornice, in which the loopholes, etc., are cut quite through the whole thickness of the wood."

The mouldings of the wainscotting in the Long

[1] Of these Mr. Gotch writes: "The curious infelicity which dogs much of the work of Elizabeth's time is apparent here, the great badges in the frieze being out of all scale with the work above and below."—*Architecture of the Renaissance in England.*

Geo. Cross, Photo]

PANELLING IN THE LONG GALLERY.

Gallery are not worked on the solid, as in other parts of the house, but are planted on. The woodwork exhibits all the refinements of modern joinery, but the more finished workmanship becomes less substantial and shows more signs of decay than the earlier work. The door is apparently in two separate thicknesses fixed together, making it about two inches thick, but the secrecy of a mortice lock had apparently yet to be discovered. The carving in the panels no longer stands out in relief as in the Dining Room, but consists of patterns formed by sinking the groundwork and leaving the design on a level with the face of the panel.

In the autumn of 1888 a spirited discussion took place in the columns of *The Athenæum* as to the original appearance of the panelling of the Long Gallery at Haddon Hall. It was occasioned by permission having been granted to Dr. Furnivall by the Duke of Rutland to remove from a portion of the wainscoat the thin coat of paint with which the oak is covered. This he proceeded to do, with results that may be still seen on the door and adjoining panels on the north side of the room. The controversy turned on the question as to whether the coat of paint was original and co-eval with the woodwork itself, or whether it had been applied at some later time. Dr. Furnivall's plea was that the painting was "an act of barbarism," put on probably only "a hundred or more years ago," and that its removal was simply restoring the oak to its real state. But the evidence all went to show that the woodwork had been intended to be painted originally, and that if the present thin wash on the panels is later in date it probably replaces earlier painting. It is indeed impossible to believe that the flat panels between the pilasters were intended to be left in bare oak.

In *The Builder* for March 2, 1889, Mr. J. Hungerford Pollen thus described the appearance of the wainscot: "The panelling of this room is of oak, as that species of timber was abundant in former days on most estates in England. The whole surface has been, at some period, washed over with a light distemper coat, once probably white, now ash grey, over which the workman has laid a sort of graining of foxy red, now faded. This graining is not done by ingenious combings, wiping out of veins, etc., in the modern manner. It has been dashed on by a rapid stroke of a broad washing brush spread out with the fingers, beginning from the bottom of the panel, carried up to the top, round, and down again. At first sight one might suppose it to have represented sweet cedar, then a rare wood. It differs from the more careful solid painting in oil, with pickings out of gold, which decorates the panels of some other rooms in the house, and has every appearance of a rapid freshening-up for some festive occasion."

In the steward's accounts, under date 1640, is a

J. R. Wigfull, Photo]

FIREPLACE IN THE LONG GALLERY.

payment for "painting the gallery," which probably refers to the wainscot and ceiling. But whether or not the woodwerk had been painted previous to this date we can only surmise.

The hue of the panelling in the gallery is faded, but the natural silver grey of the old oak showing through what remains of the paint on its surface, gives a delicate tone to the panelling, which, if unpremeditated, is none the less beautiful in itself.

There is only one fireplace in the Long Gallery, which to our modern ideas seems quite inadequate. The chimney-piece is remarkably plain and unpretentious for Elizabethan work, having something of the well developed classic character of a later day. It is in stone, but stands flush with the wall, and in no way emphasises the position of the fireplace as was usual at this period. Above the chimney-piece is a large painting said to represent Thomyris, Queen of the Massagetæ,[1] presented with the head of Cyrus; a copy from Rubens. The brass fire-dogs are curious. They stand on goat's feet, and are decorated with human heads and heads of goats. The grate is similar to that in the drawing-room.

[1] Thomyris was Queen of the Massagetæ. After her husband's death she marched against Cyrus, who wished to invade her territories, cut his army to pieces, and killed him on the spot. The barbarous queen ordered the head of the fallen monarch to be cut off and thrown into a vessel full of human blood, with the insulting words of *satia te sanguine quem sitisti.* Her son had been conquered by Cyrus before she marched herself at the head of her armies.—*Lempriere's Classical Dictionary.*

In a glass case on the window-sill at the end of the room is a cast of the head of Grace, Lady Manners, wife of Sir George Manners, and foundress of the Grammar School at Bakewell. It is said of her that "either from being afraid of not being made sufficiently beautiful on canvas, or from some other cause, she would never have her portrait painted, and that therefore after death this cast was taken."

From an inventory taken in 1623 we find among the items of furniture of the Long Gallery at that time a long table and a cupboard, a large number of chairs and stools in black and red velvet and satin, a green couch, a great number of window cushions in various colours, principally red and green, twelve carpets, "pictures little and great," and "at the gallery door a cupboard and a viall chest with a bandora and vialls." In 1637-8 there were in the Long Gallery "a gilded orgaine," "3 large harpiscalls with frames to stand on," "a shovel-board table with 5 tressalls," "a large looking glasse of 72 glasses," and "4 pictures of sheapeards and sheaperdesses." At a still later date, in 1641 (the year after "painting the gallery"), the items of furniture in this apartment are given as follows:

"The organ.

Two Harpsicalls with frames.

A great picture over ye Chimney.

Two Couches with silver and coloured leather.

Twenty backe Chaires of ye same, all covered with Blew bayes.

One great Chaire, two Cushions with tassells, one foote stoole of greene velvett imbrodred with gold and fringed with gold.

ffive Turkie Carpetts.

One great glasse.

The pictures of a Sheppard and Sheppardesse.

Eight guild Armes, with Socketts."

ANTE-ROOM.

From the upper end of the Long Gallery a doorway opens into a small Ante-Room, formerly designated the ORANGE PARLOUR. This forms part of the eastern range of buildings which are older than the Gallery itself. The walls are wainscotted up to within four feet of the ceiling with plain square panels, and have recently been hung with tapestry. From this room a doorway leads by a flight of steps on to the Terrace, or Winter Garden. Tradition says it was through this doorway and down these steps that Dorothy Vernon passed on the night of her elopement. The door, however, as we have seen, is of much later date than the room, and was probably inserted when the Terrace was laid out in its present form. In 1649-50, about ninety years after the marriage of Dorothy Vernon to John Manners, this doorway is designated "the new door made out of the Orange Chamber." The tapestry in the ante-room is a set of hangings known as The Acts of the Apostles. There are three pieces—(1) Conversion of St. Paul, (2) Shipwreck of St. Paul, (3) Deliverance of St. Peter from Prison.

It is under this ante-room, in the thickness of the wall between it and the Long Gallery, that the remains of a spiral stone stair may be seen. The stairs stop against the floor of the Long Gallery, showing that the original arrangement of this end of the eastern buildings was different, or was intended to be different, from what it now is.

STATE BEDROOM.

The State Bedroom is twenty-six feet long by twenty-one feet wide, and is lighted on the west side by a large bay-window overlooking the upper courtyard. This bay-window is a later addition to the original room, which, according to Jewitt, was formerly known as the Blue Drawing Room. It is raised two steps, and measures ten feet across the opening. The floor of the bedroom is of concrete. As in the ante-room, the walls are wainscotted with plain square panelling and hung with tapestry. The frieze is embellished with the arms and crests of Manners and Vernon. The fireplace is in stone, and, though plain, is more Elizabethan in character than that in the Long Gallery. Above it is a curious bas-relief representing Orpheus

J. R. Wigfull, Photo]

FIREPLACE IN THE STATE BEDROOM.

charming the beasts, described variously as "a fine example of pargetting," and "a clumsy composition of rough plaster." In the fireplace is a grate somewhat similar to those in the Drawing Room and Long Gallery and a pair of fire-dogs in brass and iron.

The hangings are a set of Mortlake tapestry, known as The Five Senses (Hearing, Feeling, Seeing, Tasting, and Smelling), with medallions in the borders representing subjects taken from Æsop's Fables. The lower border of each bears a scroll with the motto "Sceptra Fovent Artes." The tapestry was restored in 1898 by Miss Gemmell, of London. The pieces are as follows:

1. Hearing. Border (left): The ass in the lion's skin; (right) The fox and the stork. (Between entrance and window.)
2. Smelling. Border (left): The fox and the stork; (right) The dog and his shadow. (Between bed and fireplace.)
3. Tasting. Border (left): The fox dining with the stork; (right) The stork dining with the fox.
4. Seeing. Border (left): The wolf and the crane; (right) The dog and the wild boar.
5. Feeling. Border (left): The fox and the grapes; (right) The ape and the fox.

The State Bed is of large dimensions, and measures 14 feet 6 inches in height. It is draped with green silk velvet and white satin, embroidered and enriched with needlework. It is said to have been the work of Eleanor, wife of Sir Robert Manners, and eldest sister and co-heiress of Edmund, Lord Roos, in the reign of Henry VI. She died in 1487. The bed is reported to have been taken to Belvoir on the occasion of the visit of the Prince Regent, afterwards George IV., who was the last person to occupy it. It was afterwards sent back to Haddon.

Other articles of furniture now in the State Bedroom include a wooden cradle, in which all the Manners down to Duke John were rocked," two chairs, a table, and a spinet. In the window recess is hung a handsome looking glass, described as "Queen Elizabeth's mirror," and in a glass case are preserved some relics and curiosities connected with Haddon. The most interesting of these is a Washing-Tally, of which an engraving is given by Mr. Jewitt, whose description may be quoted: "This very interesting relic, which is of the time of Charles I., and of extreme rarity, is 5½ inches in length, and 4½ in depth. It is formed of a piece of beech wood, a quarter of an inch in thickness, covered with linen on back and sides. Its construction is that of a 'Hornbook.' In front the names of the different articles of clothing are printed from a copper plate and protected by a sheet of horn. Around the edge a narrow strip of thin brass, fastened down with highly ornamented

THE STATE BED.

nails, attaches the horn, the paper, and the linen to the wood. The 'tally' is divided into fifteen squares, in each of which is a dial numbered from 0 to 12, and above each square is the name of the article of clothing intended to be taken into account. These are 'Ruffes,' 'Bands,' 'Cuffes,' 'Handkercher,' 'Capps,' 'Shirtes,' 'Half-shirtes,' 'Boote-hose,' 'Topps,' 'Sockes,' 'Sheetes,' 'Pillowberes,' 'Table-clothes,' 'Napkins,' and 'Towells.' On each of the dials is a circular brass indicator, fastened by a little pin in its centre, so as to be turned round at pleasure. Each indicator is pierced on one side, close to the edge, with a round hole, through which one number only on the dial is visible at a time, and opposite to this hole is a raised point by which the indicator can be turned as required."

Beyond the State Bedroom, up two steps, is an apartment known as the Ancient State Bedroom, which contains a very interesting set of Lambeth tapestry hangings, representing The History of Vulcan. There are six pieces, which are as follows:

To the right on entering—1, Vulcan spreading the net; 2, Vulcan and the gods; 3, Mars and Venus; 4, Cupid standing by an anvil (probably a fragment from "Vulcan and Cupid"); 5, Fragment of "Vulcan forging" (over fireplace); 6, Neptune appealing to Vulcan on behalf of Mars and Venus (incomplete).

Eight steps lead from this room to a wide landing where, standing against the wall, is an ancient Rack for Stringing Bows. It consists of two upright pieces of wood pierced with holes and forming a kind of strong framework, and was attached at the top to the wall and at the bottom to the floor.

OTHER ROOMS.

From this landing the visitor passes to the spiral stone staircase which leads to the summit of the North-East Tower. This portion of the building is very old, and the rude workmanship offers a striking contrast to the refined elegance of the rooms just left behind. The tower rooms do not require any description. There are three apartments one over another over the gateway, in the middle one of which may be seen, on the outside wall facing east, the inner side of the corbel table mentioned on page 55. It is nine inches above the floor, and projects ten inches from the wall.

From the North-East Tower the visitor retraces his steps to the old Orange Chamber, and leaves the Hall by "Dorothy Vernon's Door."

It is from the North East Tower that the best view of the Upper Courtyard is obtained. The visitor is not taken into the courtyard, though when the door behind the screen in the Great Hall is open he may make a hasty inspection of it from that point. In size it is less than the lower courtyard,

THE NORTH-EAST TOWER FROM THE UPPER COURTYARD.

its dimensions being about eighty feet by seventy feet. The entrance is in the north-east corner under the tower, which from the courtyard presents a very bold aspect. The watch turret springing directly from the ground has an appearance of greater height than when viewed from any other point. This was the principal entrance to the Hall in the old days. The hill falls very steeply outside till the gate is reached, and under the archway the slope of the ground is considerable, but the surface of the courtyard itself, which is of gravel, falls very slightly. The west side, opposite the entrance, is occupied by the Great Hall with a single window similar to those facing the lower courtyard, and a pointed doorway opening on to the screens. In the angle to the left is the square bay formed by the staircase from the Great Hall, balanced in the opposite angle by a similar bay, one of the few indications at Haddon of symmetry and balance in design. On the south side is the Long Gallery with two windows. The east side is bounded by the earlier buildings of the fifteenth century with the later added bay-window, while along the north are continued the range of northern apartments belonging to the last building period at Haddon Hall. The character of the masonry sufficiently indicates the extent of each of these different sections. With the exception of the Great Hall all the rooms round the upper courtyard on the ground floor appear to have been cellars or offices, although to one, that under the state bedroom, the name "gymnasium" has been given.

The apartments other than those mentioned above, can only be seen by special permission. They therefore require less description. The visitor may, however, console himself with the knowledge that all that is best worth seeing, and everything of general interest, is shown him. Edward King, in his quaint description of Haddon Hall, published in 1782, dismisses the rest of the house in these words: "All the rest of this great pile of buildings is filled with small trifling apartments, not one of which deserves description, but which form a labyrinth almost as inextricable as that of Crete, and which could be of no use but to lodge a vast *host* of dependents, retainers, and servants."

There are, however, one or two rooms in the northern range of buildings that warrant more attention than Mr. King was disposed to bestow.

Of the three Rooms in the North-West Tower the two lower are interesting apartments wainscotted in oak and with ornamental plaster ceilings. The wainscot of the apartment immediately over the entrance is perhaps more distinctly Elizabethan than that in any other part of the house. The walls are divided vertically by pilasters, and the space between is filled with large panels deeply moulded. The frieze and cornice of the pilasters is continued round the room, but not the surbase.

The ceiling is divided into four compartments by moulded and ornamented beams, in each of which is a large foliated quatrefoil. This room is lit on three sides by windows facing north, west, and to the lower courtyard. The apartment above is somewhat similar in appearance, but the wainscot has all been recently renewed, retaining, however, some of the old panels. The square shape of the room is broken by an entrance screen in one corner. The ceiling is again divided into four compartments, but the ornamentation is less rich. Both these ceilings are given among the measured drawings in Mr. Duesbury's supplement to Rayner's work. The topmost room is supposed to have been a place of confinement ("the chamber called Oxford Gaol," see p. 64), because the bars and bolts were on the outside of the doors only. It has two windows with stone seats, and a door on to the leads. The door on to the leads, however, hardly suggests a prison.

In the central portion of the northern range are three interesting rooms, known respectively as Dorothy Vernon's Room, Roger Manners' Room, and Lady Cranbourne's Chamber. DOROTHY VERNON'S ROOM, situated over the great kitchen, is a large but low apartment hung with tapestry and panelled in oak. There are five hangings representing hunting scenes, and a sixth with a figure in armour. This piece is coarse in workmanship, and "might have been made by an amateur at home."[1] The figure cannot be identified, but "considering the inferior workmanship of this hanging there must have been something in its history to entitle it to its present position."[2] The oriel window in the angle of the kitchen chimney, which forms so picturesque a feature on the north front of the building, lights Dorothy Vernon's Room, and is not less charming inside than out. The oriel recess, as well as the whole of the outside wall of the room, is panelled in oak, and this is continued round the recess of the long low five-light window that lights the room at the other end. The floor in the window recess is slightly raised and a seat two feet wide is formed on each side of the opening. This is a delightful old room, though rather dark, and suffering, like many other rooms at Haddon, from disuse. No fires are lit in any part of the house in winter.

Roger Manners' Room and Lady Cranbourne's Chamber are situated on the first floor of the northern range of buildings between Dorothy Vernon's Room and the North-West Tower. Both rooms have windows facing north, and Roger Manners' Room is further lighted by two windows to the lower courtyard and Lady Cranbourne's

1 Kerry's *Derbyshire Tapestry*.

2 The tradition is that it was woven by Mary Queen of Scots, and represents James V.; the letters at the bottom standing for I(ames). Y. S(cottis).

Chamber by a two-light window overlooking a small area, or well. A special emphasis is given in these rooms to the doorways, windows, and fireplaces, each of which, being panelled above or below in oak, forms a composition by itself, the wall space between being hung with verdure tapestry from ceiling to floor. Lady Cranbourne's Chamber still retains its old oak window shutters. The pierced metal casement fasteners in Roger Manners' Room should be noticed. These rooms derive their names from Roger Manners, brother of Sir John Manners, the husband of Dorothy Vernon, and from Margaret, daughter of the eighth Earl of Rutland (d. 1679), and wife of James, third Earl of Salisbury and Viscount Cranbourne.

"Before leaving here," wrote Mr. R. Morrison Marnock, "let us notice how it is that the effect of much of this work is so exceedingly picturesque, especially, perhaps, in the window. The proportion of solid to opening gives a result of light and shadow which we can admire, but not with reason adopt. In a room 9 feet high, as we have here, to put a window scarcely 4 feet high, and the head of that nearly 2 feet 6 inches below the ceiling line, is sufficient explanation for the work being more attractive than our own. They appear to have considered windows as only to be tolerated; hence their smallness and their charm. We, on the other hand, have to deal with large openings, often equal in area to the piers with which they alternate, these openings, moreover, being filled in with a polished and unbroken surface of glass, which in itself is enough to mar a picturesque effect in our modern architecture."[1]

From Lady Cranbourne's Chamber a picturesque WOODEN GALLERY with oak balusters crosses the little area or well before mentioned, forming a communication with the first floor rooms in the older centre portion of the house west of the Great Hall. This little gallery forms one of the most charming "bits" of Haddon Hall.

The northern apartments are approached by two principal staircases. One is that leading from behind the screen at the end of the Great Hall. Another entrance is from the lower courtyard by the door immediately to one's left when facing the porch of the Great Hall. At the end of the passage a short staircase turns right and left to Roger Manners' Room and Lady Cranbourne's Chamber. These stairs deserve notice. They are somewhat curiously contrived, and their details are good. There is another staircase in oak, from the first to the second floor, on which signs of the original gilding can still be traced. It is plain in detail, but the steps, as in the other staircases at Haddon, are cut angleways out of solid blocks of timber.

The room over the buttery is known as the NURSERY. It has a gabled roof with the ceiling

1 *The Building News*, 16th April, 1875.

OPEN GALLERY. NORTHERN APARTMENTS.

about half way up the slope. The walls are hung with four pieces of tapestry, belonging to the set of the Story of Diana. They are—(1) The slaughter of Niobe's children by Diana and Apollo, (2) Diana imploring Jove for permission to remain for ever the Virgin Queen, (3) Diana with bow and arrows, (4) Diana resting from hunting.

In the adjoining room to the north (BEDCHAMBER IN BAY) is another piece belonging to the set of the Story of Diana representing Diana and Meleager. This room also contains two fragments from the Life of Alexander between the windows, and two borders by the door. It is lit by three windows to the lower courtyard of two lights each.

From the Nursery six steps lead up to the MINSTRELS' ROOM over the porch. The room contains a picture of the Entombment of Christ, but is otherwise bare.

In the Upper Courtyard are several Basement Rooms worthy of notice. On each side of the entrance gateway are rooms with arched ceilings and walls of immense thickness, which may have been part of an anterior building. On the northern side of the courtyard is what appears to have been the Bakehouse (pistrina, or "pastry") with its huge fireplace and ovens. The room under the state bedroom was, according to Mr. Jewitt, used in later times as a gymnasium for the family. The basement of the Long Gallery is divided into a series of cellars by walls and partitions. It is impossible to identify their uses. That under the central portion, including the square bay, is said to have been the Armoury, and the rooms between this and the dining-room appear to have been used as washing houses.[1] These basement walls are of immense thickness, the splays to the bay-windows measuring nearly nine feet.

The Western Range of Buildings is thus described by Mr. Jewitt: "On the ground floor, next to the so-called Chaplain's Room, were two waiting-rooms; and then the steward's room, next to the chapel entrance; over this entrance the steward's bedroom,[2] approached by a spiral staircase near the belfry tower, from a closet in which access is gained to the leads. . . . Then on this first floor are a bedroom, the "barmaster's room," the evidence room, and another bedroom, which brings us back to the entrance gateway."

1 Jewitt.

2 This was the real Chaplain's Room.

[*Geo. A. May, Photo*]

"DOROTHY VERNON'S WALK."

CHAPTER IV.—THE GARDENS.

We need not wish these gardens as they were,
With yews all clipped and t rtured, and square beds
Bordered with chiseled stones. See how the roots
Of the old trees have burst their narrow bounds,
And kicked away the stones with scornful feet.

P. G. HAMERTON.

The Gardens at Haddon are not very extensive, owing to the circumscribed area of the available site. It is, however, quite inaccurate to state, as did Bishop Kennet, that the house has "no manner of prospect, no walks or gardens.' The garden front of Haddon Hall as seen from the terrace, and the terrace as seen from the Upper Garden, are views that are so well known and so deservedly admired that no further praise of them is necessary.

The Gardens lie on the south and south-east sides of the house, and were probably finished by Sir John Manners, the husband of Dorothy Vernon, the main lines of formerly existing gardens being no doubt followed. The terrace balustrade and steps, and the steps to "Dorothy Vernon's Door" without question show the Manners influence, and are the only indications of the spirit of the Renaissance in the exterior of Haddon Hall.

The natural irregularities of the ground are responsible for the rather unusual form in which the gardens at Haddon are laid out. These irregularities, however, have been made use of in a most happy fashion by forming the gardens in a succession of terraces down the side of the hill.

"I cannot refrain from noticing," says Mr. Duesbury, "the extreme artistic skill with which the irregularities of the ground are made use of and the gardens are laid out. They consist of bold lines and terraces, which harmonize with, carry out, and add dignity to, the lines of the building, and, as house gardens always should, they form an integral portion of the design."

The gardens are laid out at four different levels on the hillside. There is first what is known as DOROTHY VERNON'S WALK, or The Rookery, a broad avenue, shaded from one extremity to the other by lofty sycamore trees, which forms a kind of upper terrace. "In springtime," wrote Mr. Cokayne, "the pathway and banks on either side in this avenue are a magnificent natural carpet of aconites, and when in full bloom the effect is gorgeous." This upper walk, which is not very well known to visitors, is reached by a flight of fifteen steps nearly opposite "Dorothy Vernon's Door."

On the next level is what is termed the WINTER GARDEN, in which the visitor finds himself on leaving the Hall. The Winter Garden is divided into three parterres, enclosed by stone kerbs, and planted with yew trees. These were once clipped, but are now grown into great trees overshadowing the entire terrace.[1] Nothing, however, could be finer than the effect produced by the trees as they

[1] *The Formal Garden*, by Reginald Blomfield.

Geo. A. May, Photo]

THE TERRACE WALK.

now stand, with the massive background of the lofty sycamores of Dorothy Vernon's Walk. The Winter Garden is 180 feet long and about 80 feet wide, part of it extending along the eastern side of the house. From the ante-room of the State Bedroom the doorway known as "Dorothy Vernon's Door" opens on to the Winter Garden. It is so called from the prevailing tradition that through it the lady passed on the night of her elopement. The door is, of course, of later date. In the steward's accounts "from Michelmas, 1649, to Michelmas, 1650," it is called the "new door made out of the Orange Chamber," a name by which the ante-room was then known. The following entries from these accounts seem to show that a bowling green then occupied the site of the Winter Garden, or some portion of it.[1]

"Paid Thos. Scattergood, Henry Smedlie, John Smedlie, George Smedlie and Hindman for getting stone and making a new wall beginning at the new door made out of the Orange Chamber and so following the upper side of the Bowling Alley round about to the Stand, being in measure 88 roodes made at 11s. the rood.	48 8 0
"Paid Thos. Scattergood for hewing stones for garden doors and making the same doors against the stand.	9s. 4d.

[1] Edward King, as late as 1782, mentions "a sort of small bowling green" upon one of the "terrasses" of the garden.

"Paid the same Scattergood for setting the stairs with old steps betwixt the bowling alley and upper walk."	13s. 4d.

This seems to refer to the enclosing wall of the Winter Garden and the steps to Dorothy Vernon's Walk. The Stand was no doubt at the end of the Terrace, and was an erection for spectators, occupying the place of the modern summer house, which is built on the remains of the old Stand. This entry shows, at any rate, that work was being done in the gardens as late as 1650.

The Winter Garden is separated from the Upper Garden by the well-known terrace balustrade. The TERRACE, which is 120 feet in length, runs at right angles to the house, a position for which the irregularities of the site are responsible, and from it the finest view of the south front of Haddon is obtained. The balustrade runs flush with the end of the Long Gallery. There are five bays, or compartments, at each side of the steps, with six small stone arches to each bay. The piers are surmounted by balls, and are 11 feet 6 inches from centre to centre. The height of the balustrade is three feet. "The terrace at Haddon," says Mr. Gotch, is "as good an example as can be found of the fine effect of a raised walk approached by a broad flight of steps, and protected by an arcaded balustrade. The detail is quite simple, there is no particular effort visible, everything seems to

J. R. Wigfull, Photo]

THE WEST FRONT FROM THE RIVER.

be there because it is wanted, but the whole effect is extremely picturesque."[1]

From the terrace a flight of twenty-six steps leads down to the UPPER GARDEN. This is the principal garden of the house, and extends along the greater part of the south front. It is 120 feet square. The eastern side is bounded by the terrace wall and steps, while on the south and west it is built up from the hillside by sturdily buttressed walls. The garden is laid out as a lawn, with a broad gravel walk running round it and up its centre. On two sides are hedges of box and yew, and in one corner are the remains of an old sundial, dated 1591. The difference of level between the Upper and Winter Gardens is only about ten feet.

From the Upper Garden a gravelled path leads by the side of the building to the chapel. There is a drop of five steps opposite the dining-room bay, and further on by the chapel two more drops of thirteen and six steps respectively. This brings one to the landing at the top of the long flight of seventy-six steps on the left, which descends to the old footbridge over the river. The LOWER GARDEN lies between these steps and the Upper Garden. It is roughly terraced down the hillside from north to south, and is approached from the steps at different levels. It has long been in a very wild

1 *Early Renaissance Architecture in England*, by J. A. Gotch, p. 133.

state, having apparently had little attention paid to it, but is now being brought back to cultivation.

Near the summit of the hill above Haddon is the Bowling Green, occupying an acre of ground. The approach is by an avenue of lofty trees, which leads to the entrance gateway. There is a flight of sixteen steps with a balustraded wall on either side. At the far end is a lodge, or summer house, which bears, on a lead rain-water head, the date 1696, under an Earl's coronet. Rayner says: "This building appears to have been handsomely fitted up, and it was nearly finished when the noble founder removed from Haddon." The Bowling Green is now converted into a garden, and the lodge is used as a dwelling. The entrance gateway and walls have been recently restored.

This bowling green appears to have taken the place of the one previously mentioned as existing in the Winter Garden. King speaks of a "more modern" green having been formed up the hill, "supported by walls built round it, like a sort of hanging garden, and having a large summer house adjoining."

North of the Bowling Green may still be seen the site of the Archery Ground—an open space in the wood approached by an avenue of lofty trees.

Geo. A. May, Photo]

ENTRANCE TO BOWLING GREEN.

CHAPTER V.—THE LORDS OF HADDON.

"Let wealth and commerce, laws and learning die,
But leave us still our old nobility."—
England's Trust and other Poems, 1841.

The more notable of the lords of Haddon have been already mentioned in the first chapter. It will therefore not be necessary to give more than a chronological list of the names of the owners of Haddon Hall from the twelfth century down to our own day.

The PEVERELS (*c.* 1086 to *c.* 1154). The reader desiring further information concerning this family than is given in the first chapter is referred to the article "Peverell" in the Dictionary of National Biography, and to Mr. J. R. Planché's paper on "The Family of Peverel of Nottingham" in the Journal of the British Archæological Association, Vol. VIII.

The AVENELS (*c.* 1154 to *c.* 1190).

RICHARD DE VERNON[1] (*c.* 1190), married Avicia Avenel. To him was issued the licence to strengthen, but not fortify, his house at Haddon. He was living in 1215, but dead before 1219.

1 For the Vernon genealogy see "*Haddon: The Hall, the Manor, and its Lords*," by W. A. CARRINGTON, in the "Derbyshire Archæological and Natural History Society's Journal, vol. xxii.

William de Vernon, son. Twice married. Living in 1236. Died about 1242.

Sir Richard de Vernon, son. He was living in 1276. Died without issue.

Robert de Vernon, brother. He is supposed to have died shortly after Richard. The descent of Haddon terminated in the male line with this Robert, who appears to have died without male issue, leaving an only daughter, Haweis, who married

Sir Gilbert le Franceys. Little is known of him. He was dead in 1278, and was succeeded by his son Richard, born in 1261, who assumed his mother's name, and is known as

Richard de Vernon. He married Isabel, daughter of Sir William Gernon, of Bakewell. He was apparently alive in 1323, in which year his son died.

William de Vernon, grandson. He was born in 1314, but the date of his death is unknown.

Sir Richard de Vernon, son. He married Juliana, sister and heiress of Sir Fulk de Pembrugge, lord of Tong, in Shropshire. Tong was for many years after this the burial-place of the Vernons. He died in 1376.

Richard de Vernon (1376-1400), son. Born about 1368. Married Johanna, daughter of Rees ap Griffith.

Sir Richard de Vernon (1400-1450), son. Born

VERNON QUARTERING AVENEL.

1st and 4th Argent, a frett, sable (Vernon), 2nd and 3rd Gules, six annulets, argent (Avenel).

CREST OF VERNON.

CREST OF MANNERS.

1390. He was Treasurer of Calais, Captain of Rouen, and Speaker in the Parliament at Leicester in 1426. He married Benedicta, daughter of Sir John Ludlow, of Hodnet, Shropshire. His name, with that of his wife, is on the glass in the east window of the chapel. Monument at Tong.

Sir William de Vernon (1450-1467), son. He had a grant of the office of Knight Constable of England for life. He married, in 1435, Margaret, daughter of Sir Robert Pype and Spernore. Brass at Tong.

Sir Henry Vernon (1467-1515), son. Born 1441. He was governor and treasurer to Arthur, Prince of Wales, son of Henry VII. He married Anne Talbot, daughter of the Earl of Shrewsbury. There is a chantry and monument at Tong. His eldest son, John, died in his father's lifetime (1477), and is buried in Bakewell Church.

Richard Vernon (1515-1517), son. Born about 1485. He married Margaret, daughter of Sir Robert Dimock. Monument at Tong.

Sir George Vernon (1517-1567), son. He was the last male of the Vernons who dwelt at Haddon, and was known as The King of the Peak. He married (1) Margaret, daughter of Sir Gilbert Talboys, and (2) Maud, daughter of Sir Ralph Longford. He left two daughters, co-heiresses, to one of whom, Dorothy, the Haddon estates passed after his death. He is buried at Bakewell.

Sir John Manners (1567-1611), the husband of Dorothy Vernon, was the second son of the first Earl of Rutland. He was knighted in 1603, after his wife's death. Buried at Bakewell.

Sir George Manners (1611-1623), son. He married Grace, daughter of Sir Henry Pierrepoint. She founded the school at Bakewell. Buried at Bakewell.

John Manners (1623-1679), son. On the death of his cousin, the seventh Earl of Rutland, who died childless, he succeeded in 1641 to the Earldom, and thus united the two lines of the Manners family. Belvoir Castle, in Leicestershire, the seat of the Earls of Rutland, thus passed into the same ownership as Haddon, and the family alternately resided at one or the other. During the Civil War the Earl of Rutland resided chiefly at Haddon. He married Frances, daughter of Lord Montague of Boughton.

John, 9th Earl and 1st Duke of Rutland (1679-1711), son. He had been created a peer in his own right[1] just before his father's death in 1679, and in 1703 he was created Marquis of Granby and Duke of Rutland. He married three times. He died at Belvoir.

1 As Baron Manners of Haddon. The title has since been held by the successive peers under the Dukedom. In 1896, the Marquis of Granby, eldest son of the present Duke was, however, summoned to the House of Lords, where he now sits as Lord Manners of Haddon. The two titles are, therefore, at present (1904) distinct.

ARMS, CREST, &c., OF THE DUKE OF RUTLAND.

Or., two bars Azure; a chief quarterly of the second and Gules, the first and fourth charged with two fleurs de lis of the first, and the second and third with a lion passant-guardant of the same, being an augmentation given to the family in consequence of their descent from King Edward IV.

Crest: On a chapeau, Gules, turned up Erm., a peacock in pride, proper.

Supporters: Two unicorns, Arg., their horns, manes, tufts, and hoofs, Or.

Motto: Pour y parvenir.

John, 2nd Duke of Rutland (1711-1721), son. He had married in 1693, when seventeen years of age, the second daughter of Lord William Russell, by whom he had nine children. She died in 1711. He afterwards married the daughter of Lord Sherard, by whom he had eight children.

John, 3rd Duke of Rutland (1721-1779), son. He had thirteen children, nearly all of whom died young. He lived partly at Haddon, but it was during his life that the family finally quitted the house. The Duke was familiarly known as "Old John of the Hill" and lived to the age of eighty-three. His eldest son, who predeceased him, was the celebrated Marquis of Granby, Commander-in-Chief of the British Forces in Germany during the Seven Years' War.

Charles, 4th Duke of Rutland (1779-1787), grandson. He was the son of the Marquis of Granby. "He was an early and always a staunch friend of the younger Pitt, for whom he obtained a seat in Parliament in 1780. On the formation of Pitt's administration in 1783 he became Lord Privy Seal, and in the following year Lord Lieutenant of Ireland, where he died in 1787, at the early age of thirty-three." His correspondence with Pitt has been published. He married a daughter of the Duke of Beaufort.

John Henry, 5th Duke of Rutland (1787-1857), son. He was nine years of age when he succeeded his father. He married, in 1799, Lady Elizabeth Howard, daughter of the Earl of Carlisle. He pulled down Belvoir Castle, built by the eighth earl, and erected the present building. He received the British Archæological Association at Haddon in 1851.

Charles, 6th Duke of Rutland (1857-1888), son. He entertained the Prince and Princess of Wales to luncheon at Haddon in 1872. He took little part in public affairs, and was unmarried.

John, 7th Duke of Rutland (1888), brother, the present owner of Haddon. As Lord John Manners he had a long parliamentary career extending over nearly half a century. He was First Commissioner of Works in Lord Derby's administration of 1852, and he held the same office in 1858-9, and again in 1866-7, when he had a seat in the Cabinet. He was Postmaster General from 1874 to 1880, and again in 1885, and in Lord Salisbury's administration of 1886 he took office as Chancellor of the Duchy of Lancaster. He was born in 1818.

CHAPTER VI.—THE TOMBS IN BAKEWELL CHURCH.

> "Old moniments, which of so famous sprights
> The honour, yet in ashes, did maintain."

It is hardly possible to conclude a notice of Haddon Hall without some reference to the tombs in the Vernon Chapel at Bakewell Church. The chapel was erected about 1360 upon the walls of a former chapel, but was pulled down and rebuilt in 1841, and now comprises the Chapel of Our Lady and the Vernon Chapel. It is on the east side of the south transept, and within it lie buried the later Vernons and the earlier members of the Manners family connected with Haddon.

The earliest of the Vernon monuments is the small alabaster altar tomb of John Vernon, son of Sir Henry Vernon, who died in 1477. Until 1881 this tomb was in the centre of the chancel.

The fine altar tomb of Sir George Vernon stands in the middle of the chapel against the east wall, more to the north than its original position. It bears the recumbent effigies of Sir George and his two wives, and is a fine and characteristic example of early Elizabethan work. Along its sides are shields of arms of the Vernons and their alliances, and those of the families of the two wives on the north side. The shields are held by the three heiresses who were married to members of the Vernon family. The figure of the knight is in plate armour and surcoat, with straight hair and a long beard. The wives are dressed precisely alike, in long black robes and close fitting caps. The inscription has never been finished, the blanks for the dates not having been filled in.

Against the wall at the south end of the chapel stands the monument to Sir John Manners and his wife Dorothy Vernon. It is a large and pretentious structure in the later Elizabethan style. Under an arch in the centre are the kneeling figures of Sir John and his wife facing each other. Between them is a pedestal with an inscription. Above this, under the arch, is a large shield of sixteen quarterings, Manners impaling twelve quarterings of Vernon. On the top of the cornice are two obelisk-shaped ornaments, and between them a large shield bearing the sixteen quarterings of Manners. Below the principal figures, in the base of the monument, are the figures of the four children who were the issue of the marriage.

Against the north wall of the chapel is the monument to Sir George Manners and his wife Grace Pierrepoint. The monument is not in its original position. Till 1841 it stood over the tomb of Sir Thomas de Wendesley, forming the division between the Vernon Chapel and the Chapel of Our Lady. It is similar in style to that of Sir John Manners, but is larger and more ambitious. In the centre of the monument are the figures of the knight and his lady kneeling at a lectern. Behind the figures is a tablet with a long inscription in Latin. On the top of the monument is a shield with the sixteen quarterings of Manners as on the opposite monument, and below the principal figures are effigies of the nine children of the marriage arranged in two rows in arched niches, each bearing an appropriate motto.

The remaining tomb in the Vernon Chapel is that of Sir Thomas Wendesley, Knight, of Wendesley in the Parish of Darley, who was mortally wounded at the battle of Shrewsbury in 1403. The tomb on which the effigy is placed is modern. Sir Thomas married the Lady Juliana, widow of Sir Richard de Vernon, and was buried in the Chapel of Our Lady just outside the Vernon Chapel.

Against the east wall of the chapel is a small mural alabaster monument to John Manners, third son of Sir John Manners and Dorothy Vernon, who died in 1590, aged fourteen years.

All these monuments are described at great length, and with much attention to their heraldry, by Dr. Cox in his *Churches of Derbyshire*, Vol. II. He also gives an interesting description of the uncovering of the remains in the Vernon Chapel at the time when it was reconstructed in 1841. To the visitor to Bakewell, however, to whom Dr. Cox's work may not be available, the account of the monuments given by the late Mr. Cokayne in his handbook *A Day in the Peak*, is recommended.

A BIBLIOGRAPHY.

Sequel to the Observations on Ancient Castles. By EDWARD KING. In vol. vi. of "Archæologia," 1782, pp. 346-359.

Magna Britannia. Vol. v. Derbyshire. By D. and S. LYSONS. 1817.

The History and Antiquities of Haddon Hall. By S. RAYNER. 2 vols. 1836.

Supplementary Number to Rayner's Haddon Hall. By HENRY DUESBURY. 1837.

Haddon Hall in the Olden Time, and a description of the Mansion in 1838.

Mansions of England in the Olden Time. First Series. By JOSEPH NASH. 1839. Plates xxi. to xxv., "Haddon Hall."

Views of Haddon Hall. By DOUGLAS MORISON. 1842. 26 drawings, without text.

Haddon Hall. By HENRY DUESBURY. In the Journal of the British Archæological Association. Vol. vii. 1852.

Haddon Hall. By LLEWELLYNN JEWITT, F.S.A. Reprinted from "The Stately Homes of England."

A Day in the Peak: an illustrated Handbook to Bakewell Church, Haddon Hall, and Chatsworth. By A. E. COKAYNE.

A Short Account of Haddon Hall. By J. ALFRED GOTCH. (Illustrated by THOMAS GARRATT). 1889. Reprinted from "The Builder," January 12th, 1889.

Haddon Hall, being Notes on its History. By the DUCHESS OF RUTLAND. Reprinted with additions from "The Quarterly Review," January, 1890.

The Old Halls, Manors, and Families of Derbyshire. By J[OSEPH] T[ILLEY]. Vol. 1. The High Peak Hundred. 1892. "Haddon Hall," pp. 5-8.

Haddon Hall. Illustrated by W. E. COOKE. 1892 48 drawings, without text.

Descriptive Notes on the Tapestry in Haddon Hall. By LADY VICTORIA MANNERS. 1899.

Architectural and Historical Notes on Haddon Hall. By F. H. CHEETHAM.

Selections from the Steward's Accounts preserved at Haddon Hall, from 1549 to 1671. By W. A. CARRINGTON.

Article *Peverell (William)* in "The Dictionary of National Biography." By W. E. RHODES. Vol. xlv., p. 134.

Article *Vernon (Sir Richard de),* in "The Dictionary of National Biography. By G. LE GRYS NORGATE. Vol. lviii., pp. 279-280.

On the Armorial Bearings of the families Ferrars and Peverel. By J. R. PLANCHÉ. In "The Journal of the British Archæological Association," vol. vii.

The Family of Peverel of Nottingham. By J. R. PLANCHÉ. In "The Journal of the British Archæological Association," vol. viii.

The Chapelry of Haddon. By Dr. J. CHARLES COX. In "The Churches of Derbyshire," vol. ii., pp. 87-94.

Haddon: The Hall, the Manor, and its Lords. By W. A. CARRINGTON. In "The Derbyshire Archæological and Natural History Society's Journal," vol. xxii.

The Painted Windows in the Chapel of S. Nicholas, Haddon Hall. By the Rev. CHAS. KERRY. In "The Derbyshire Archæological and Natural History Society's Journal," vol. xxii.

Sixteenth Century Woodwork. Illustrated from Haddon. By R. MORRISON MARNOCK. In "The Building News," April 2 and 16, 1875.

Correspondence relative to the Woodwork at Haddon Hall. In "The Athenæum," August 25th, September 1st, 8th, and 22nd, 1888. By A. HARTSHORNE, Dr. FURNIVALL, Dr. J. CHARLES COX, A. E. COKAYNE, CHARLES FERGUSON, and Prof. T. ROGER SMITH.

The Woodwork of Haddon Hall. By J. HUNGERFORD POLLEN. A letter to "The Builder," March 2nd, 1889.

An Old House. By ARTHUR T. BOLTON. In "The Builders' Journal," January 28th, 1896. (Illustrated.)

Inscriptions graven on Old Panes of Glass at Haddon. By the DUCHESS OF RUTLAND. In "The Queen," November 27th, 1897.

Haddon Hall. By ARTHUR J. PENTY. In "The Builders' Journal," August 29th, 1900. (Illustrated).

Haddon Hall in Print. By F. H. CHEETHAM. In "The Builders' Journal," September 10th, 1902.

Gardens Old and New: Haddon Hall. In "Country Life," June 1st, 1901 (Illustrated.)

The Gardens at Haddon Hall. By F. H. CHEETHAM. In "The Builders' Journal," October 7th, 1903. (Illustrated).

Haddon Hall: Royal Institute of British Architects Extra Silver Medal Drawings, 1887. By FRANK BELLIS. In "The Building News," February 11th, 18th, and March 11th, 1887.

Haddon Hall [A Poem]. By P. G. HAMERTON. In "The Isles of Loch Awe." 1855.

Peak Scenery, or Excursions in Derbyshire. By E. RHODES. 2 vols. 1818-19.

The Peak Guide. By STEPHEN GLOVER. 1830. "Haddon Hall," pp. 82-103.

The Gem of the Peak. By W. ADAM. 1843.

The Peak of Derbyshire. By J. LEYLAND. 1891. (Drawings of Haddon by HERBERT RAILTON).

Domestic Architecture of the Middle Ages. By J. H. PARKER. Vol. iii., part 2. "Haddon Hall," pp. 220-222.

Architecture of the Renaissance in England. By J. ALFRED GOTCH. 2 vols. 1894.

Early Renaissance Architecture in England. By J. ALFRED GOTCH. 1901.

A History of Renaissance Architecture in England, 1500-1800. By REGINALD BLOMFIELD. 2 vols. 1897.

INDEX.

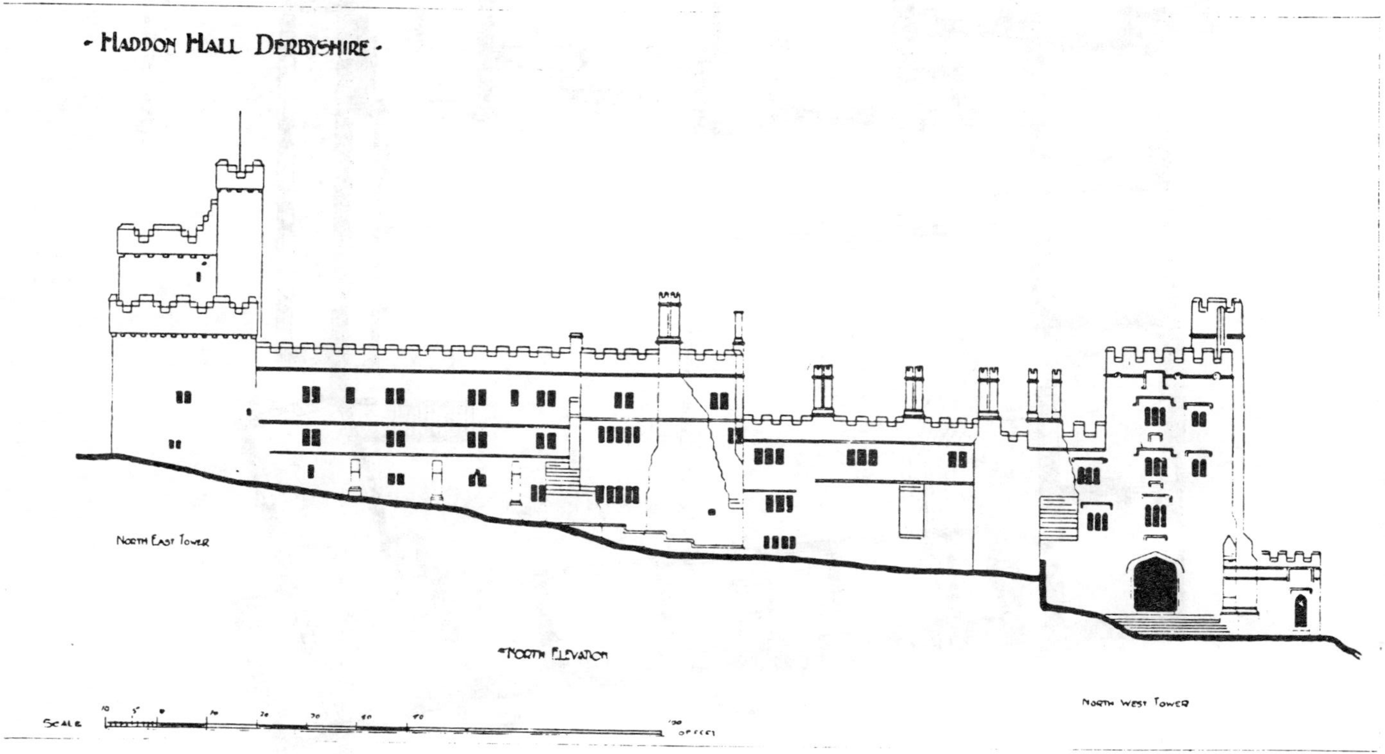

THE NORTH FRONT, SHEWING SLOPE OF HILLSIDE.

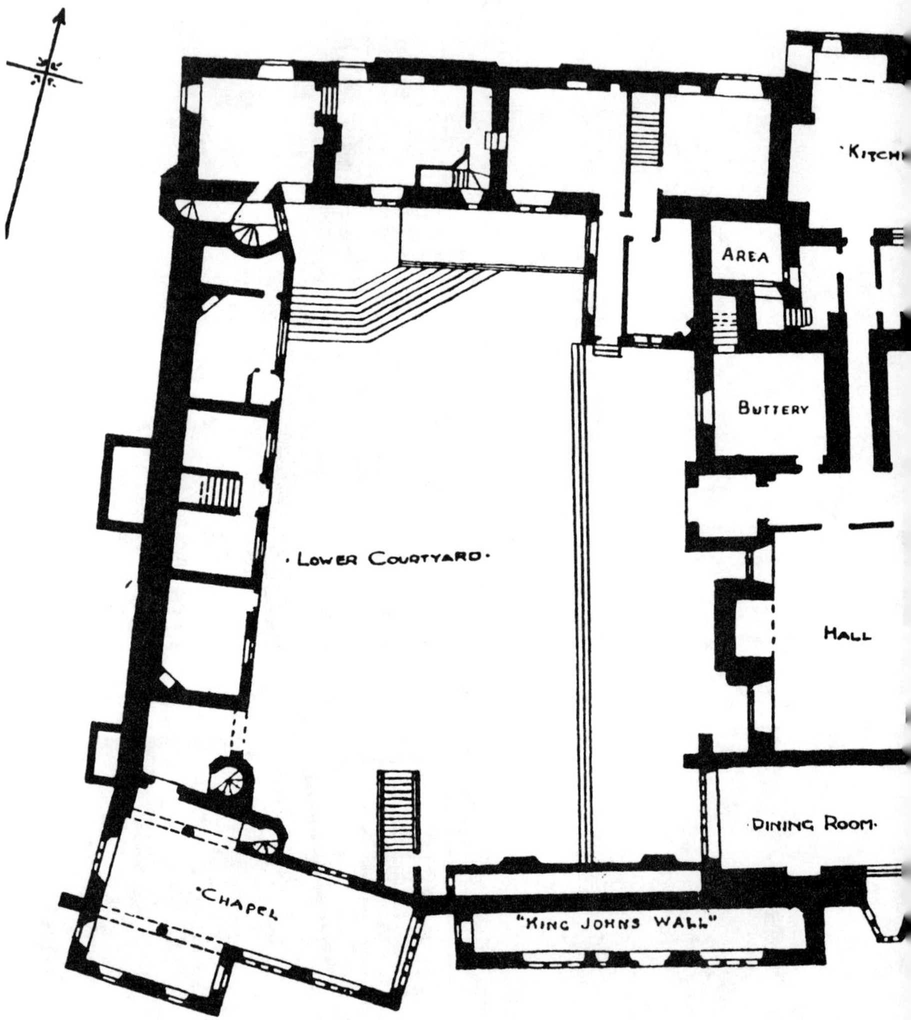

·Kitch
Area
Buttery
·Lower Courtyard·
Hall
·Dining Room·
·Chapel
"King Johns Wall"
Scale
10 5 0 10 20 30

· Haddon Hall, Derbyshire ·

· Ground Plan ·

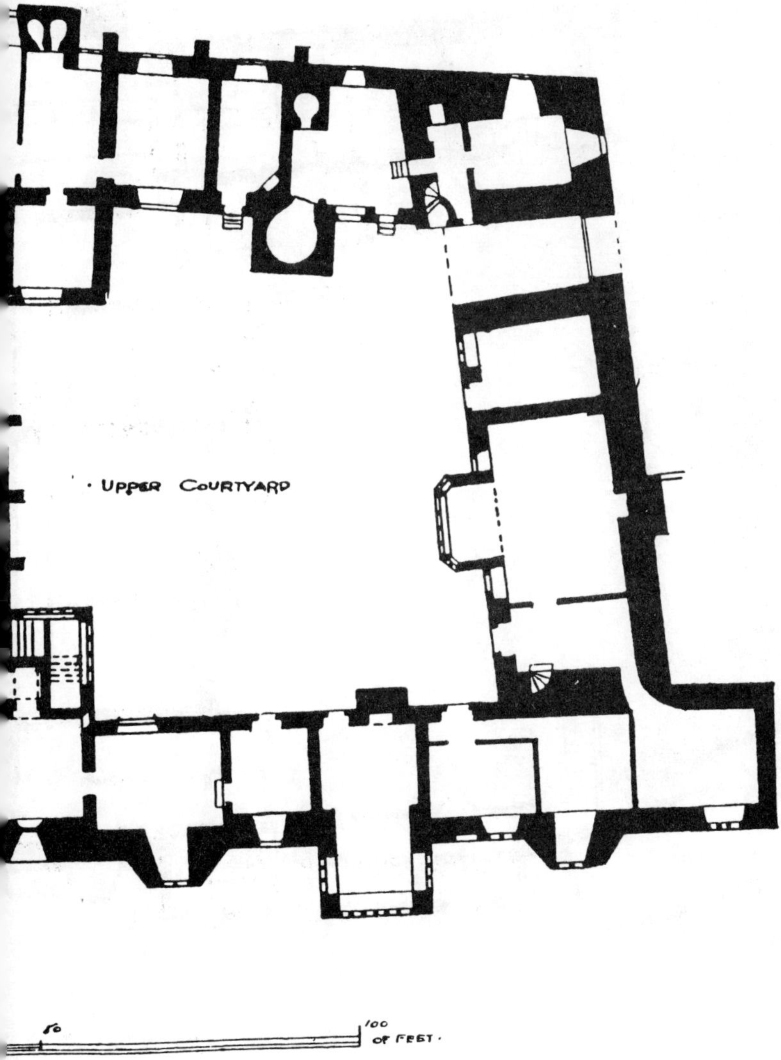

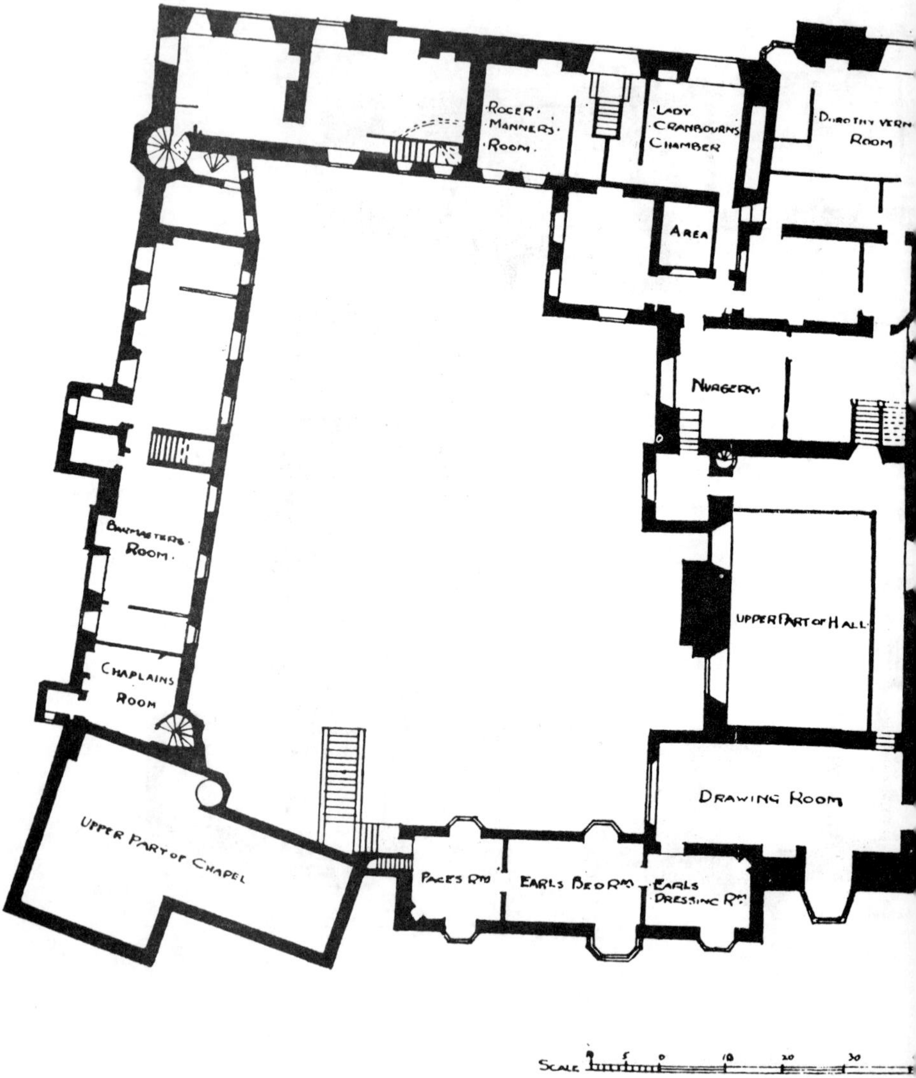
Roger Manners Room
Lady Cranbourns Chamber
Dorothy Vern Room
Area
Nursery
Bannisters Room
Upper Part of Hall
Chaplains Room
Drawing Room
Upper Part of Chapel
Pages Rm
Earls Bed Rm
Earls Dressing Rm
Scale
10
20
30

· HADDON HALL, DERBYSHIRE ·

· FIRST FLOOR PLAN ·

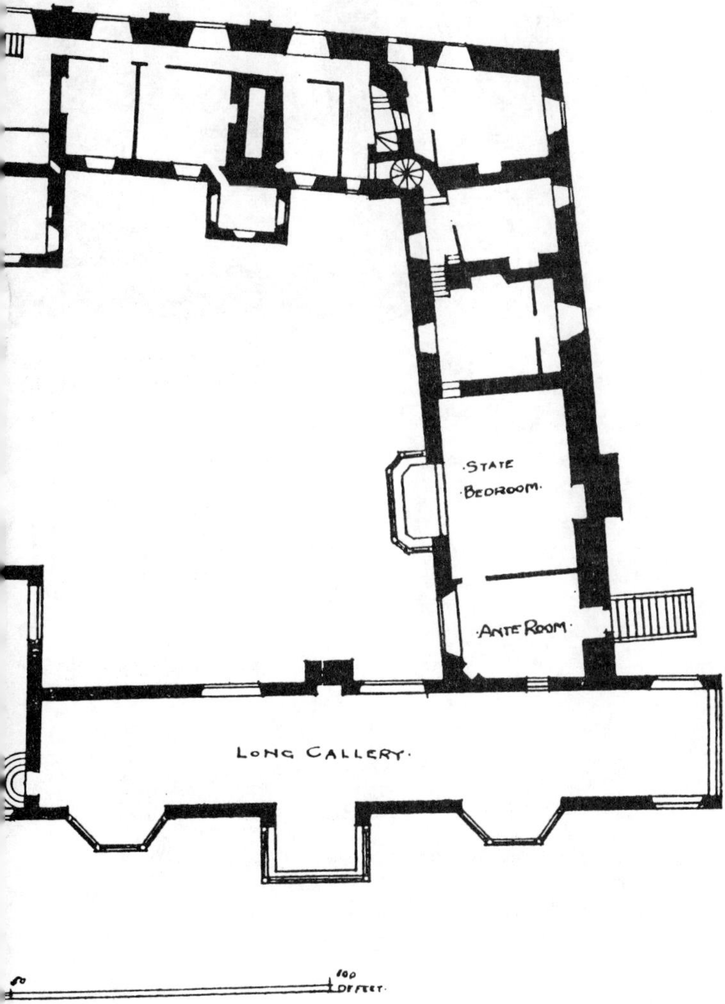

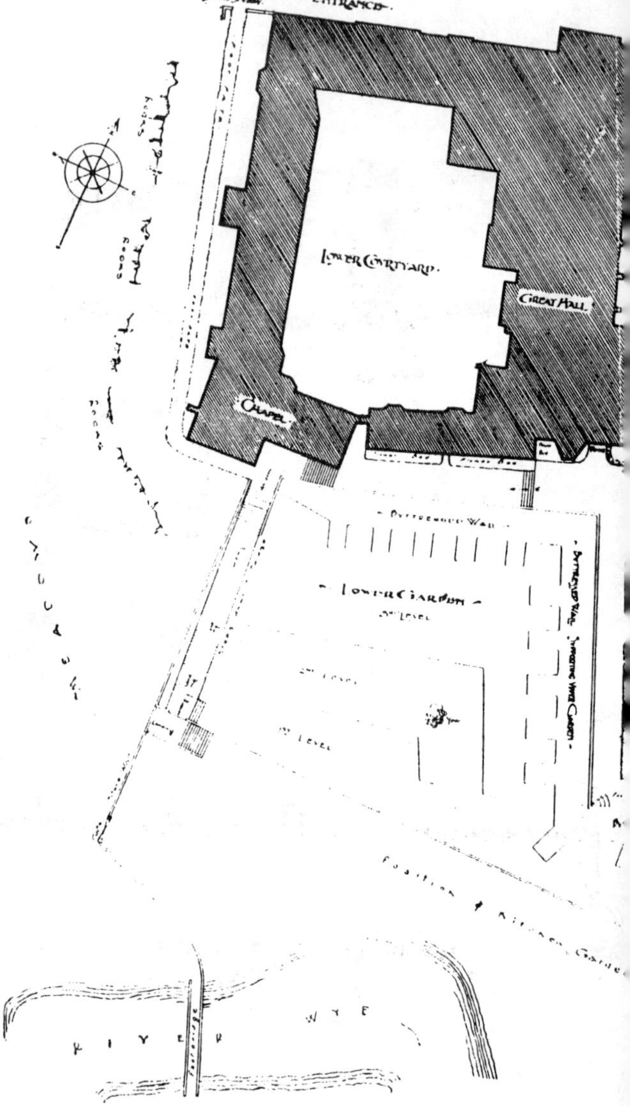

From Measureme

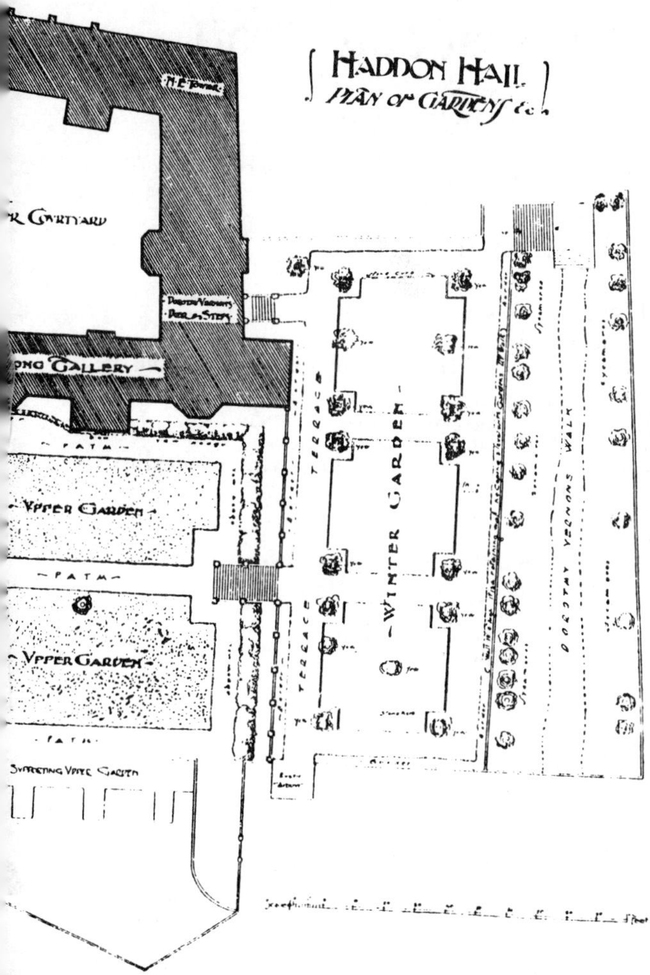

ken in May, 1902.